THE STORY OF
TEACHING

A lesson in grammar

THE STORY OF
TEACHING

MARTIN BALLARD

PHILOSOPHICAL LIBRARY

Published, 1971, by Philosophical Library Inc.
15 East 40th Street, New York 16, New York.

Copyright © 1969 by Martin Ballard

SBN 8022 2067 3

━━━━━━

To
GRACE ALLEN HOGARTH

Printed in Great Britain by
Lowe & Brydone (Printers) Ltd., London

Contents

Acknowledgements

THE AUTHOR wishes to express his thanks to Dame Kitty Anderson for advice and help with Chapter 7.

The publishers gratefully acknowledge permission to reproduce the following illustrations in this book: The Metropolitan Museum of Art, Rogers Fund, 1916 (p. 5); Radio Times Hulton Picture Library (pp. 7, 34, 63, 84); Governors of Sherborne School (p. 8); Landesmuseum, Trier (p. 11); Houghton Mifflin Company, from *History of Education* by E. P. Cubberly (pp. 13, 37); Greater London Council Photograph Library (pp. 17, 18, 52, 82, 83); The Mansell Collection (pp. ii, 24, 51); B. T. Batsford Ltd, from *The English Public School* by M. V. Ogilvie (pp. 27, 28); The John Hilleson Agency Ltd (p. 31); R. Levinson, Ben-Shemen, by courtesy of Routledge & Kegan Paul Ltd, from *Education in Israel* by J. S. Bentwich (p. 36); S. C. Moreton-Prichard (p. 41); Dover Publications, Inc, New York, from *Old-Time Schools and Schoolbooks*, by Clifton Johnson (p. 57), reprinted through permission of the publisher; from *The Lancastrian System of Education with Improvements* by Joseph Lancaster, Baltimore, 1821 (p. 61); The Libraries Committee of the Royal Borough of Kensington and Chelsea (p. 70); Governors of the North London Collegiate School (p. 73).

The publishers are also grateful for permission granted by the following: Harmony Music Ltd, from 'What Did you Learn in School Today' by Tom Paxton (p. 3); J. M. Dent & Sons Ltd, from Plutarch's *Life of Cato* (p. 4) and *Émile* by Rousseau (pp. 78, 79); Longmans Green & Co Ltd, from *The Secret of Childhood* by Maria Montessori (pp. 17, 83); George Weidenfeld & Nicholson Ltd, from *The Hothouse Society* by Royston Lambert (p. 21); Sheed & Ward Ltd, from *A History of Education in Antiquity* by H. I. Marrou, trans. Manon (p. 22); The Clarendon Press, Oxford, from *The Republic of Plato* trans. F. M. Cornford (p. 25); Kensington Music Ltd, from 'Ha, Ha, Thisaway' by Huddie Ledbetter (p. 33); George Allen and Unwin Ltd, from *Education and the Social Order* by Bertrand Russell (p. 42); Methuen & Co Ltd, from *The Life of Galileo* by Bertolt Brecht, trans. Desmond I. Vesey (p. 44); Harper & Row Inc, from *Erasmus* trans. Preserved Smith (p. 69); The Society of Authors as Agents for the Bernard Shaw Estate (p. 77); University of London Press Ltd, from *Readings in the History of Educational Thought* ed. Cohen & Garner (p. 82); Hart Publishing Company, New York, from *Summerhill: A Radical Approach to Child Rearing* by A. S. Neill, 1960 (p. 86).

Table of Dates and Events
Significant to the Story of Teaching

B.C.

c. 3000	Early developments of writing and scribal education in China, Egypt and Sumeria; Phoenician alphabet
c. 800	Development of Judaic traditions
c. 470	Socrates born in Greece
c. 450	Sophists flourishing in Greece
460–431	Athens at the height of its glory
404	Sparta at height of its power
399	Socrates died
388	Plato (c. 428–348) established his Academy
384	Demosthenes born in Greece
335	Aristotle (384–322) founded Peripatetic School in Athens
322	Demosthenes died
234–149	Cato the Elder lived in Rome
106–43	Cicero lived in Rome
27	Roman Empire established by Augustus

A.D.

95	Quintilian (35–95) wrote his *Institutio Oratora* describing the education of an orator and analysing the elements of a classical speech
313	Constantine the Great legalized Christianity by the Edict of Milan
c. 400	Monastic education began in England
413–426	St Augustine (354–430) wrote *City of God*
476	Western Roman Empire collapsed
800	Charlemagne I crowned Emperor of the West
871–899	Alfred the Great ruled as King of Wessex
1279–1292	Roger Bacon (1214–1294) confined by the Franciscans for his heretical propositions

1382	Winchester College founded
14th c.	Beginning of the Renaissance in Italy
1440	Invention of movable type in Germany
1453	Muhammed captured Constantinople; end of Byzantine Empire; Grand Seraglio set up
1492	Discovery of New World by Columbus
1509	John Colet founded St Paul's School
1516	Thomas More (1478-1535) wrote *Utopia*
1519	Erasmus (1466-1536) wrote his *Colloquies*
1522	Martin Luther (1483-1546) translated New Testament into German
1525	William Tyndale translated New Testament into English
1527	Dr Lily's Latin Grammar published
1534	Ignatius Loyola founded the Jesuit order
1536	John Calvin (1509-1564) published *Institutes of the Christian Religion*
1539	End of monastic education in England
1547	John Knox (1505-1572) began preaching Calvinism in Scotland
1552	Christ's Hospital founded
1597	Francis Bacon (1561-1626) published *Essays*
1598	Gresham's College founded in England
1618–1648	Thirty Years' War in Germany
1633	Galileo (1564-1642) forced to renounce his theory of the universe
1641	Comenius visited England
1642	Compulsory science teaching established in Saxe-Coburg-Gotha
1647	Massachusetts Law passed to provide primary education for mass of the population
1649–1660	Commonwealth in England
1686	Charles Morton emigrated to America

1729   John Wesley (1703–1791) became leader of the methodist society in Oxford; Methodism is usually dated from this time

c. 1770   Industrial Revolution began in England

1743   Benjamin Franklin (1706-1790) proposed that English replace classics as focus of education and that science be added to the curriculum in American schools

1762   Jean-Jacques Rousseau (1712-1778) published *Emile*

1763   Compulsory state education established in Prussia

1771   Rev. Francis Asbury sent to America by Wesley to establish the Methodist Church there

1789-1799   French Revolution

1798   J. H. Pestalozzi (1746-1827) opened his school for destitute children in Switzerland

1801   Joseph Lancaster opened his first monitorial school in England

1803-1815   Napoleonic Wars

1826   F. W. A. Froebel (1782-1852) published *The Education of Man*

1828-1842   Thomas Arnold headmaster of Rugby

1837   Froebel opened the first kindergarten in Switzerland

1838   Oberlin College in America admitted women

1837-1848   Horace Mann Secretary of Board of Education in Massachusetts

1839   First Normal School for training teachers opened in Lexington, Massachusetts

1848   Queens College, Harley Street founded

1850   North London Collegiate School founded by Frances Mary Buss

1853   Cheltenham Ladies College founded

1857   Thomas Hughes published *Tom Brown's Schooldays*

1858–1906	Dorothea Beale headmistress of Cheltenham
1859	Charles Darwin published *The Origin of Species*
1861	Herbert Spencer (1820–1903) published *On Education*
1862–1938	Henry Newbolt
1862	Payment by results and graded tests of literacy introduced in English schools
1870	English Primary Education Act set up state schools; provided for non-denominational religious instruction; instituted School Boards at primary level
1871	Kennedy's *Public School Latin Grammar* published
1872	Kalamazoo Michigan judgement asserted the provision of high schools was a valid use of public money
1896	John Dewey established Laboratory School, Chicago
1900	Mr Justice Wills pronounced against higher grade schools in England
1900	Sigmund Freud (1856–1939) published 'The Interpretation of Dreams'
1902	English Education Act established scholarships to grammar schools
1906–1909	Maria Montessori (1870–1952) founded her teaching Method
1921	A. S. Neill (1885–) founded Summerhill
1925	Stopes 'Monkey' Trial in Dayton, Tennessee
1944	R. A. Butler Education Act
1948	U.S. Supreme Court act barred religion from state schools
1957	Russia launched Sputnik I; US stepped up technological education
1964	Comprehensive reorganisation began in English education
1967	Plowden Report
1968	Newsom Commission Public Schools Report

Introduction

IT would be hard to choose any more massive subject on
which to write a short book than *the story of teaching*. If
one were writing the history of electrical engineering or
insurance, the scope would at least be confined to the
activities of a clearly defined group of people within a
limited period of history. The story of teaching, however,
has no limits. Even the most primitive society evolves some
method of passing information and attitudes on to its
children, and the advanced societies in which we live spend
a substantial proportion of the earnings of industry and
commerce on training the rising generation.

Teachers sometimes complain that those outside the
profession do not treat their art with the respect afforded to
medicine or the law. Doctors and advocates have in some
measure succeeded in preserving their trades as 'mysteries',
shut off from the enquiring eyes of laymen. In contrast, every
man in the street considers himself qualified to offer advice
on what should happen within the walls of a classroom. This
need cause no surprise. Education is rightly the concern of
the whole community, and all members of society, from
parents to politicians, have a vested interest in it. The
teacher is, therefore, bound to work under conflicting
pressures from the world outside the school, and his task
will be influenced by the needs of the society which he
serves.

It is clearly impossible to offer anything like a complete
history of education within the scope of a very short book.
The following chapters, therefore, isolate just a few of the
demands which society has placed upon the educational
process, and show the way that teachers have reacted to
them in changing situations. Even with this limited aim,

vast areas of the subject have to be omitted. The scope is limited to that part of the teaching process which can be included in the term 'schooling', and illustration is generally drawn from the elements which have been influential in forming the English speaking tradition. No attempt is made to include university or adult education as these are full-scale studies in their own right. The chapters are arranged in themes rather than on a chronological basis. A chart is therefore provided so that readers can check how particular events fit into the over-all time pattern.

The book is intended for those with no academic background in education, and especially for young readers. It is, however, impossible to tackle such a subject without broaching some difficult concepts. The story of teaching degenerates into a series of meaningless anecdotes the moment it is divorced from its background in scholarship and abstract ideas. This book is written from the point of view of a working teacher, not of an expert in the theory of education, and the author has made no attempt to disguise his point of view on important issues. He is aware of the many pitfalls which await anyone who embarks on a short work on such a large subject. If, however, there is material interesting—and provocative—enough to stimulate further thought and reading, his purpose will be well served.

1. Teaching the Warrior

What did you learn in school today, dear little boy of mine?
What did you learn in school today, dear little boy of mine?
I learned that war is not so bad.
I learned about the great ones we have had.
We fought in Germany and in France
And some day I might get my chance.
That's what I learned in school today;
That's what I learned in school.

TOM PAXTON

THE word to *teach* can be used in two ways. In our society it is commonly used to describe a professional activity. In this sense, a teacher is a person who earns a living by passing on some form of knowledge or skill. We can, on the other hand, apply the word in a much looser sense. Everyone is in some measure a teacher. A mother shows her child how to use a knife and fork; a father teaches him to fly a kite or hold a spade.

In the second, broader meaning of the word, the human race shares the ability to teach and learn with other higher mammals who care for their young and show them how to adjust to their environment. No human being is without teachers; the accomplishments we learn at school are only a part of the whole process of learning, which begins in infancy and continues throughout life. The term *education*, however, is generally reserved for the more formal process in which young people are prepared in a deliberate way to fulfil their role in society. We talk of illiterate peasants as being 'uneducated', because they have never shared in this activity. They take their place beside their parents in the fields as soon as they are old enough to wield a hoe, and their life is a continuous struggle to grow the bare necessities for survival. Education is a luxury which they cannot afford,

3

and for which they have no obvious use.

After many generations the farmers of a society begin to produce small quantities of surplus food and a favoured group of men emerges, for whom survival is not the sole motivating force in life. If the society is in danger of attack from neighbours, this leisured class becomes a warrior aristocracy with responsibility for the defence of the common people who provide the food.

It is in the training of these warriors that the story of teaching may be said to begin. If a man is to stand firm on the battlefield in the face of death he must be taught to overcome his natural instincts by a rigid discipline of mind and body. The main ingredients of a warrior's training have remained remarkably constant in widely separated civilizations and over many centuries. Plutarch describes how Cato, in ancient Rome, looked after his son's training:

He himself, therefore, taught him his grammar, law and his gymnastic exercises. Nor did he only show him too how to throw a dart, to fight in armour and to ride, but to box also and to endure both heat and cold, and to swim over the most rapid and rough rivers. He says, likewise, that he wrote histories, in large characters with his own hand, so that his son, without stirring from his house, might learn to know about his countrymen and forefathers.

Thus like an excellent work, Cato formed and fashioned his son to virtue; nor had any occasion to find fault with his readiness or docility; but as he proved to be of too weak a constitution for hardships, he did not insist on requiring him any very austere way of life. However, though delicate in health, he proved a stout man in the field.

Very few Roman parents were as diligent as Cato in teaching their children the military virtues, but his was the ideal to which they all paid lip service. Lip service, however, was not enough. The community became exposed to its enemies the moment the training of the warrior class was neglected, and in some societies the state took this responsibility away from the parents.

The Spartans set about the task in a ruthlessly methodical manner. The whole community was orientated to warfare. There was no place for weaklings, so unfit infants were carried on to the hillside and left to die; the rest were taken from their parents and brought up with complete dedication

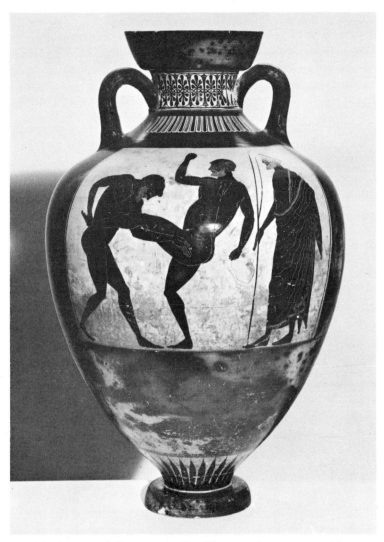

Athenian vase, fifth century B.C.: Two wrestlers are engaged in a
Pankration while the trainer with stick looks on

to the ideals of physical fitness and service to the state. The
very codes of right and wrong were dictated by the demands
of warfare. Since the soldier in the field had to forage for
food as best he could, Spartan children were taught how to
steal and to lie. An action only became morally wrong when

it was found out. A well-known story recounts how a boy
was stopped, carrying a stolen fox. He hid the creature
hurriedly under his tunic and showed no sign of pain while
it gnawed at his chest. Without warning he fell down dead
as it bit into his heart. It was a story that could be told with
pride; the boy had shown the spirit which inspired Leonidas
and every one of his 300 Spartans when they died in the
Pass of Thermopylae. It was the end product of a long
process of self-denial and physical exercise.

It is common today to look upon the working man as
'tough' and the aristocracy as 'feeble'. In the Middle Ages,
however, it was the nobleman who was trained in physical
prowess. To be killed in battle by a common soldier was the
ultimate indignity for a knight. He too had been taken
from his family at an early age, and sent to live in the house-
hold of a nobleman. There the master of the henchmen
taught him to ride and wear armour. He learned to hold a
lance and to joust at the tournaments, until he was finally
able to follow his lord into battle as a squire.

Purely physical training, however, was not enough. The
warrior's mind as well as his body had to be conditioned for
the ordeals ahead. Cato wrote histories 'in large characters
with his own hand so that his son might learn to know about
his countrymen and forefathers'. Every warrior had to be
steeped in the past glories of his people so that he would
readily sacrifice his own life to maintain the tradition. It is
an obvious fact that there are as many battles lost as there
are battles won; yet even today a child following a school
history course is led to believe that his national story is
strewn only with victories. English children learn of Agincourt in 1415 and Blenheim in 1704, and are never told that
English arms failed to win a single battle of consequence
on the Continent between the two. French children never
hear of Agincourt and have but the haziest knowledge of
Blenheim.

'History should teach a patriotism which will include a
blind love of country and willing sacrifice to a greater
authority.' These words were written by Adolf Hitler in the
twentieth century, but they would have appealed to Cato
the Elder in ancient Rome. Hitler twisted the facts of
history unscrupulously to serve his own purpose and, if he

Hitler Youth: Drummers at a Party Rally

had cared to do so, he could have justified himself from an ancient tradition of education—the tradition of Homer, who wrote of the victory of the great Achilles over Trojan Hector; of Vikings, who passed the long winter nights recounting glorious deeds in blood-curdling sagas; of Japanese story-tellers, who held villagers spellbound as, with their swords flailing and their eyes ablaze, they acted out the deeds of classical heroes.

Hitler would have no physical or moral weaklings in his teaching force; the pupils of his Third Reich were to see

Sherborne School Cadet Corps in camp at Aldershot, 1906

before them only strong examples of German manhood.
His training colleges were like Spartan gymnasia, where
future teachers were conditioned for their task by a rugged
outdoor life. Such a system could 'acknowledge no truth
for the sake of truth, no science for the sake of science'.
Battles had to be won in the schoolrooms of the fatherland
and all knowledge pressed into the service of the State.

The military element in education can be seen in cultures
as far apart as the Incas and the Japanese, but it has been
particularly dominant in Western Europe where nations
have lived in a chronic state of mistrust and warfare. In
origin it is a pagan philosophy, yet it has been baptised by
the Christian Church, and found expression in the chapels
of the English public schools in scarcely less blatant a form
than in Hitler's Germany.

The mystique of the warrior scholar can be summed up
by the public school poet of the late nineteenth century,
Henry Newbolt, when he imagines taking his young son
into Clifton College Chapel and speaking, like Cato, of all
that he holds most dear:

This is the Chapel; here, my son,
  Your father thought the thoughts of youth
And heard the words that one by one
  The touch of life has turned to truth.
Here in a day that is not far,
You too may speak with noble ghosts
Of manhood and the vows of war
  You made before the Lord of Hosts.

To set the cause above renown,
  To love the game beyond the prize,
To honour, while you strike him down,
  The foe that comes with fearless eyes.
To count the life of battle good,
  And dear the land that gave you birth,
And dearer yet the brotherhood
  That binds the brave of all the earth.

My son, the oath is yours: the end
  Is His, Who built the world of strife,
Who gave his children Pain for friend
  And death for surest hope of life.
Today and here the fight's begun,
  Of that great fellowship you're free;
Henceforth the School and you are one,
  And what you are, the race shall be.

2. Teaching the Scribe

Who is there who would not recoil in horror and choose death, if he was asked to choose between dying and going back to his childhood?

ST AUGUSTINE

FIFTEEN SHEEP EIGHT BUSHELS OF BARLEY. In the early days of civilization men began to strike bargains, to pay taxes. At some point the person who handed over his sheep and barley realized that he would be well advised to get a receipt from the purchaser or tax gatherer. It occurred to someone to scratch symbols representing the goods onto a clay tablet and leave it in the sun to dry. In that way writing was born. In Sumeria, Egypt and China the art developed in picture form with symbols to represent the sheep and the barley, and then later the Persians introduced an alphabet based on sound, which was further developed in Greece and Rome into the modern western alphabet.

As soon as men started keeping written records, they found it necessary to introduce schools for training scribes. The status of the scribe has varied widely from one civilization to another. Western Europe has developed in a state of almost continuous warfare, and here he has, therefore, always been subordinate to the warrior. But in the formative stages of their development Egypt and China were not subject to severe pressure from enemies, and in these civilizations the scribes and not the soldiers rose to form the aristocracy.

The 'children of the great' went to school in the cities of ancient Egypt, where they took immense pains over the complexities of hieroglyphic writing. They worked from ancient texts, copying and recopying until they could form the letters with absolute precision. Generations of boys wrote out maxims collected in books of wisdom, like *The Teaching of Amen-em-ope*.

The scribe who is skilful in his business
Finds himself worthy to be a courtier.

Those who succeeded in reaching a high standard were able to rise to the highest posts in Pharaoh's court.

China also had a very complex script. Only pupils who combined intelligence with diligence were able to master all its subtleties. Before 2,000 B.C. the Emperor worked on the enlightened principle 'employ the able and promote the worthy'. The Great Shun examined his officers every year. After three years they were either promoted or dismissed from the service according to their results. The child who wished to rise to the top had to work his way from village school to district school, then to the college of the department, to the college of the local capital and finally to the college of the imperial capital. He had to pass a searching examination before each step in his promotion. As in Egypt, scribal education was based entirely on ancient texts. The pupil was not encouraged to think for himself, but to repeat the maxims of his forefathers. The old text could not be altered in the smallest detail, but the language in common use gradually changed, until the time came, both in Egypt and China, when the scribes were working in a dead language, and their skill became a closely guarded mystery shut off from the rest of society.

The Greeks were able to spread their education over a wider proportion of the population because the adoption of the alphabet made reading and writing a great deal easier. Scribal education did not have to be kept in a water-tight

A school lesson, from a grave-relief at Trier

compartment, and the warrior-citizen of ancient Athens could reasonably be expected to know how to read and write as well as hold a spear. In later Greek and Roman times it was the practice for all upper-class boys to go through the mill of scribal education.

In winter the boy left home before it was light, his way led by a slave (pedagogue) carrying a lamp. When they arrived at the schoolroom the slave settled down on a bench to wait, while the boy began the work of the day. He sat on a stool and chanted the letters of the Greek alphabet— alpha, alpha, alpha; beta, beta, beta. The task must have seemed endless and when it was finished the letters all had to be learned in reverse as well—from omega back to alpha. One king despaired that his son would ever master his letters, so he gathered twenty-four young slaves, named them after the letters of the alphabet and had them live continually with his son as a 'visual aid'. When the pupil had learnt his letters, he went on to syllables, starting with the easy ones, and progressing until he was ready to tackle complete words. The same pattern was followed in teaching a child to write: letters—syllables—words, until at last whole sentences crowned years of endeavour.

Fragments of school exercises have been found in the dry Egyptian sand. 'The learning of letters is the beginning of wisdom,' says one; another admonishes, 'Work hard, my lad, if you do not want a whipping.' It was assumed that no boy would learn to write without the threat of punishment. In Hebrew the words for 'education' and 'chastisement' come from the same root. When the Greek boy Coccalos played truant he was taken to his master Lampriscos who cried out,

'Where is my hard leather strap, the bullock's tail I use to beat rebellious boys. Give it to me before I lose my temper.'

'Oh, no, Lampriscos,' replies the boy, 'by the Muses and the life of your daughter Coutis, please don't use the hard strap. Use the other one instead.'

A writer who lived near a schoolroom complained that the teacher's savage threats and the sound of thrashing disturbed his morning rest.

A few questioned whether such generous use of punishment was desirable. The great Roman schoolmaster,

A Roman primary school, from a fresco found at Herculaneum

Quintilian, recorded his disapproval:

As for corporal punishment, though it is a recognized practice, I am altogether opposed to it, first because it is disgusting, fit only for slaves and undoubtedly an insult (as appears, if you change the age of the victim); in the next place, because a pupil whose mind so ill befits a free man's son as not to be corrected by reproof, will remain obdurate even in the face of blows—like the vilest of slaves; and finally, because such chastisement will be quite unnecessary if there is some one ever present to supervise the boy's studies with diligence.

Then again, if you coerce the young child by means of blows, how would you deal with the grown youth who cannot thus be driven by fear and has more important things to learn?

Now, if in choosing guardians and teachers, too little care has been taken to select those of sterling moral character, I am ashamed to mention the shameful practices for which men make this right of corporal punishment the excuse and the opportunity sometimes afforded to others too by the terror of it in the wretched child's mind. No one ought to have undue liberty in dealing with an age that is still feeble and helpless in face of ill treatment.

There is no evidence that Quintilian's views had any effect. Ordinary schoolmasters could with justice point out that he was in a position to pick and choose his pupils. Quintilian was an honoured man in Roman society and rose to the rank of consul; but most of his colleagues held too low a status to command much respect in their pupils' eyes. Some were slaves; others came from good families, but had gone down in the world. In public esteem they were graded alongside attendants at public baths, fortune tellers and tight-rope walkers. Their level of pay contrasted poorly with men in other walks of life.

> They'll give thee for thy twelvemonth's anxious pains
> As much as in an hour a fencer gains,

wrote Juvenal. He described teachers as an unhappy breed who 'perished of the same cabbage served up again and again'. Their position was low because their work demanded no skill beyond bare literacy. It was a routine occupation, drumming letters, syllables, words into unwilling skulls. The education that mattered—in the arts of war, and in the virtues of the race—went on at home, or was committed to a few selected teachers who undertook the training of the leaders of society. The ancients had no respect or love for childhood, and many would have agreed with Augustine, that it would be preferable to die than return to the deadly grind of schooling.

Despite these drawbacks, Roman parents assumed that it was worthwhile sending their sons to school. There is no way of knowing what proportion of the population could read and write, but these were by no means rare accomplishments. From the educational, as from almost every other point of view, the collapse of the Roman Empire before the Goths, Vandals, Saxons and other barbarian tribes was an unmitigated disaster. The new rulers were wild and unlettered, and their forms of government were so primitive that at first they had no need for scribes. Literacy survived precariously within the Christian Church, and, when a barbarian king wanted to send a letter to distant parts of his kingdom, he had to find a clergyman to write it, and ensure that there was a clergyman at the other end to read it. The great Emperor Charlemagne was a man of broad culture and knew both Latin and Greek yet he could not manage to shape his letters. He carried a slate and stylus round with him wherever he went, but his clerical advisers thought that he was wasting his time. Scribal skills were of no use to a ruler! He was determined, nonetheless, that learning should spread within his empire, and he gave orders that there should be study in every bishop's house and every monastery. The motto of his revival of learning was: 'Let those who can, teach.'

The enlistment of the clergy into the service of the state has left its mark on the English language. The word clerk— meaning clergyman—replaced the word scribe to describe a literate man. Through the Middle Ages, for a man to claim the privileges of a clergyman in the law courts, it was generally enough that he could demonstrate his ability to write. As trade expanded in the later Middle Ages, however, skill in reading and calculation also became desirable for merchants. The law, too, increased in complexity and became independent of the Church. Thomas More, who was successively Speaker of the House of Commons and Chancellor of England, was the first great English scholar not in holy orders. The invention of printing also made books available to a larger section of the population.

It was still assumed, however, that 'being lettered' was a special skill, required only in certain sections of society. Some religious reformers tried to extend scribal skills, but their success was limited until, in the nineteenth century, the new industries of Western Europe and America began to make increasing demands for an educated labour force. Techniques of reading and writing, once the jealously guarded preserve of a scribal class, were put into mass production for the population as a whole.

A Roman child straying into an English schoolroom some 100 years ago would have found that little had changed from his day. Everything appeared on a larger scale—up to 1,000 pupils might be sitting in one room—but the methods of teaching were substantially the same. The cane lay displayed where all could see it, as pupils sat chanting letters—syllables—words—sentences, in the time-honoured manner. Then they would take up their slates and the air would fill with squeaking as they wrote letters—syllables—words— sentences. One of the teachers might be a woman, which would cause some surprise, but the status of the job had, if possible, deteriorated. For 'a twelvemonth's anxious toil' a man received slightly more than £50, while his woman colleague had to make do with just over half that amount.

In 1862 the British government decided that greater efficiency should be brought into the system, and so a series of graded tests were introduced in the basic skills of reading, writing and arithmetic. The content of these shows how little the groundwork of education had changed since classical times:

Reading.

Standard 1. Narrative in monosyllables.

Standard 2. One of the narratives next after monosyllables in an elementary reading book used in the school.

and so on up to:—

Standard 6. A short ordinary paragraph in a newspaper, or other modern narrative.

Writing.

Standard 1. Form on a blackboard or slate, from dictation, letters, capital and small manuscript.

Standard 2. Copy in manuscript characters a line of print.

and so on up to:—

Standard 6. Another short ordinary paragraph in a newspaper or other modern narrative, slowly dictated once by a few words at a time.

The children learnt their lessons by rote, and examiners found that they could be thrown completely off balance if they were asked to start reading in the middle of a paragraph. Marks were given for accuracy rather than understanding, and for all the expression they put into the task, they might as well have been 'barking at print'.

No teacher could afford to neglect these examinations because his salary was calculated by the number of children that passed each grade. Once an able child could read the 'paragraph from a newspaper or other modern narrative' his education had finished, for the teacher had to spend any time at his disposal dragging the slower children through as many standards as they could manage.

It was still generally assumed that education was necessarily an unpleasant business, and teachers enforced their authority with the cane or strap as freely as their Roman predecessors had done. By the end of the nineteenth century, however, a number of teachers were experimenting with less painful methods of introducing children to basic 'scribal' skills. Among these was the Italian Maria Montessori who believed that there is a moment in any child's development when he is ready and willing to read. The teacher had to prepare the child with exercises—and then wait for the moment of illumination.

I was sitting near to a chimney and said to a little 5 year old boy who sat beside me, 'Draw me a picture of this chimney,' giving him as I spoke a piece of chalk. He got down immediately and made a rough sketch on the tiles which formed the floor of this roof terrace. As is my custom, with little children, I encouraged him, praising his work. The child looked at me, smiled, remained for a moment as if on the point of bursting into some joyous act and then cried out, 'I can write! I can write!' and kneeling down he wrote on the pavement again the word 'hand'.

While few would hold out the hope that all children can learn to read in such a moment of illumination, teachers now

A lesson in reading, 1905

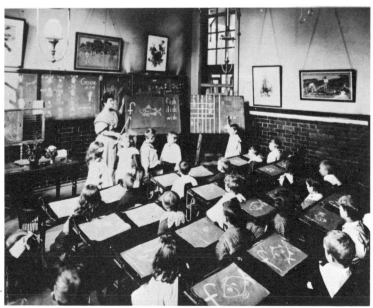

· watch for the time when their pupils are ready to approach
the task. They may, however, find themselves puzzled by the
wide difference of opinion among experts as to when this will
be. Some recommend that a child should be left untram-
meled by such cares until he is seven, while others argue that
a baby is ready to read at the tender age of two.

In recent decades the old rote methods of learning have
been generally discarded. Many children have been taught
with the Look/Say method of word recognition by which
pupils recognize a word whole, and are then expected to
transpose this knowledge to other words of similar construc-
tion. Advocates of this method point out that the ability to
read is closely linked with the ability to think, and that the
old repetition of letters, syllables, words and sentences completely fails to expand the boundaries of a child's intelligence.

The most recent research is inclined to lay the pheno-
menon of word blindness, with which secondary school
teachers are all too familiar, at the door of this Look/Say
method. Children who are never taught to split a word into
its component parts are inclined to solve spelling problems

Contemporary infants' school children learning to write

by making a wild guess rather than following logical rules. Language is a code, and a teacher has to provide pupils with a key to decipher it. This key is still to be found in the sounds of the alphabet.

Unfortunately, English-speaking children may well come to the conclusion that their particular code was invented by some malevolent adult as a refined species of torture for the young. The delight of learning becomes overlaid by frustration as a child tries to cope with distinctions between *bow* and *bough*, or to understand the logic which rejects the simple spelling *cum* for the verb to *come*.

Enthusiastic reformers argue that the rationalization of spelling would bring far greater benefits than changes in currency or units of measurement. With simplified spelling children can read earlier, write more, spell better, achieve a larger vocabulary, write more fluent creative English and suffer less frustration in the process. So far, however, there is no lobby in Parliament pressing for such a major upheaval. The whole adult population, having learnt to spell the old way, has a vested interest in preserving the status quo.

Pending such radical reform, teachers have to do the best they can to assist children to master the difficulties of the language. Some use the initial teaching alphabet, by which children begin reading on a logical system of spelling, and only tackle the anomalies of the language when they have grasped the fundamental principles of literacy. Under this method children start reading early, but naturally lose some momentum when the transition is made. Other systems use the traditional spelling, but employ colour to distinguish when combinations of letters make up a particular sound.

Recent research shows that reading problems are not simply mechanical, but can arise out of a child's home background. In some homes a little child hears a wide range of words in everyday use; in other homes he hears very few. Some children have exciting stories read to them and approach school eager to crack the code which locks up such treasures; others never learn the relevance of reading and only make half-hearted efforts to master the art because the teacher wishes them to do so.

There are some parts of the world where the ability to read and write is still the preserve of a limited scribal class.

In the developed countries, however, literacy is but the first step in the education of every child. Primary schools have the task of ensuring that children become fluent in using the symbols of their own language. Reading ages are generally creeping up, but an alarming number of children still leave school each year under an intolerable handicap. Research workers complain that the methods they evolve are not being taught in colleges or implemented quickly enough in the schools.

The public at large still looks on junior and infant teachers as being less skilled than their secondary and university colleagues. It is beyond doubt, however, that slovenly teaching in the younger age groups will do most harm in the long run. An undergraduate may complain bitterly after he has sat through a poor lecture, but he has the equipment to go away and read the subject up for himself. The little child, on the other hand, depends on the teacher for his very literacy. The peasant of past centuries suffered little, for no one expected him to be able to read. He could learn wisdom from the oral tradition of his ancestors, and from the tangible world of nature. The modern child, however, grows up in an environment programmed to a literate society, in which every person must be his own scribe. The teacher who matters most in a child's development is the one who brings him to literacy and so opens his mind to the exciting world of the printed word.

3. Teaching the Leader

Thank you, Lord, thank you for giving me the leadership of Hawthorne House; thank you for my privileges and my prefect's tie; for the house cup that we so closely won and for the trust of the boys in my house, thank you, Lord, thank you.

PRAYER OF A CONTEMPORARY ENGLISH PREP SCHOOL BOY, AGE 12

LEADING citizens of the states of ancient Greece expected their sons to grow up equipped as warriors and scribes. The time came, however, when even this was found to be inadequate preparation for the duties they would be called upon to fulfil. In fifth century Athens public life centred round the Acropolis, where free men argued about the affairs of the state. Anyone who wished to sway public opinion had to be able to organize his thoughts in a lucid manner and present them in a fluent spoken style. A group of wandering teachers, called the sophists, undertook to train young men in these qualities. When a sophist arrived in a city he would lay on a public demonstration of his teaching ability; he might deliver a formal lecture, or perhaps speak extemporarily on a theme suggested by a member of the crowd. Conventional teachers sneered at them because the whole demonstration was devised to produce the maximum effect, and they were not above a bit of sharp practice. But the art of public speaking was so valuable that pupils flocked to their schools and many sophists became rich men.

The skill which they taught was known as *rhetoric* and throughout classical times this was the one subject which had to be mastered by anyone who wished to rise to a position of influence. Demosthenes in Greece and Cicero in Rome developed public speaking to great heights of technical excellence. A moving speech delivered in the Athenian Assembly or the Roman Senate at a moment of national crisis could sway decisions and influence the course of history. Rhetoric was, therefore, the key subject for any highly-born young man. By the first century A.D., however, the political structure of the world had changed. The Greek cities had been conquered and the Roman Senate shorn of its power. Decisions were now taken by emperors and generals, who could not be swayed by the well-turned phrases of any public speaker.

Rhetoric had thus lost its practical function, but it remained the only training fit for a gentleman. It degenerated into a study of pure form, and the subject matter under consideration became unimportant. Pupils had to present logical arguments on issues such as:

Whether it is credible that a crow really perched on the head of Valerus in his duel with a Gaul, and flapped his wings in the latter's face.

When they reached a certain level of efficiency they went on to argue cases in legal form—some of which must have strained credulity to the limit:

Suppose there is a law that a priestess must be chaste and pure and her parents chaste and pure.
A virgin is captured by pirates and sold to a procurer who lets her out for prostitution. She asks her clients to pay her and yet respect her chastity. A soldier refuses to do this and tries to violate her. She kills him. She is accused of murder and is acquitted and returns home. She asks to become a priestess. Plead for and against.

It is astonishing to realize that for almost a thousand years teachers and pupils struggled their way through countless exercises of this sort. They were studying to perfect that elegant style and polished argument which were the mark of a leader of society. They took as their models the great masters of rhetoric, Isocrates and Quintilian.

As a discipline rhetoric was to have immense influence on later generations of pupils. It was still on the syllabus in the Middle Ages and returned to its old pedestal with the revival of classical studies in the Renaissance. The Italian scholar Poggio wrote to a friend describing a discovery he had made in a remote monastery:

In the middle of a well-stocked library we discovered Quintilian, safe as yet and sound, though covered with dust and filthy with neglect and age.

His friend replied in rapt tones:

So you receive the title of second author of the works you have restored to the world. Through you we now possess Quintilian entire. Before we only boasted the half of him and that defective and corrupt in text. O precious acquisition! O unexpected joy!

It is doubtful whether generations of schoolboys, set once again to construct perfect Latin following Quintilian's rules, would have joined in the chorus of joy at the discovery of the lost manuscript.

If the rhetoric of the sophists dominated the schools of antiquity, it was another Greek tradition, stemming from the philosopher Plato, which had the profounder influence on later education.

Plato was a pupil and friend of the great teacher Socrates, and he originally hoped to take his part in the political life of Athens. When the party which he supported lost power, he went into exile and set up his Academy, probably the most famous and influential school of all time. Future statesmen from all parts of the Greek world came there to learn the art of government.

Plato's long-term influence, however, came from his writings, particularly *The Republic*, in which he set out a plan of education for those who were to have charge of the affairs of state. He had no time for democracy and its handmaid rhetoric. His state was to be ruled by a select group of *guardians* who had proved themselves to be worthy of the greatest responsibility.

It is basic to Plato's thinking that everything has an *ideal*. A tree, for instance, may be stunted and deformed but there is 'in the mind of god' an ideal tree which is a standard of perfection against which all trees can be measured. In the same way there is an ideal man, and Plato's pattern of education was designed to mould the human clay as near as possible to that ideal. Those who came closest to the standard set would be the guardians of the state. He laid down the qualities that he looked for in his future leaders: they would be gentle by nature but capable of violence in time of war;

A detail from Raphael's 'The School of Athens'

they would show outstanding self-control, not be 'overmuch given to laughter', be utterly truthful—unless the reasons of state decreed that they should tell a lie. Above all their actions would be governed by a sense of duty towards the community. They would, of course, possess the qualities already noted as desirable in a warrior, and, as a bonus, they would, if possible, be endowed with physical beauty.

Like the Spartan children, the future guardians of Plato's republic were to be taken from their homes at an early age to live in a segregated community. They were never to marry but were to breed future generations of ideal citizens with female guardians under carefully controlled conditions. No mother was to know her own child, so that rulers of the state could never be tempted to found dynasties or work for the good of their families. They were to live their frugal lives openly for all to see, and, to ensure that self interest did not cloud their decisions, they were never so much as to touch silver or gold.

The education of these guardians was laid out in detail. It was to be crowned, not with the study of empty words, but by the severe discipline of *dialectic* or philosophy. In dialectic the student would rise to contemplate the ideal—the ultimate good. Only a few select individuals would reach this final stage of education, and they would be solemn citizens of 30 years of age, for:

you will see how youngsters, when they get their first taste of it, treat argument as a form of sport solely for purposes of contradiction. When someone has proved them wrong, they copy his method to confute others, delighting, like puppies, in tugging and tearing at anyone who comes near them.

Plato, an exile from his own city, was unable to put his ideas into practice, and his educational plans were soon forgotten. In more recent times, however, Platonism became a dominant influence within education.

Any attempt to construct an educational system on the lines of *The Republic* would run up against many obstacles. It would be hard to convince free men to renounce family and property ties for the sake of the state. Indeed, the only systematic attempt carried out along those lines used slaves, and may have had no direct connection with Plato at all.

When the Ottoman Emperor Muhammed conquered Constantinople in 1453 he found himself at the head of a great empire. Scarcely more than a century earlier his people had been unknown—they had no core of trained warriors or selected rulers. Somehow he had to create an élite to help him administer his dominions. He opened a school specially designed to meet this need. If Plato's Academy was the most famous school in the world's history, perhaps Muhammed's Grand Seraglio was the most remarkable. Pupils were recruited from young slaves captured in the wars. Their physique was examined carefully and they were given intelligence tests, to sort out those who would be fit to train for high office. Once inside the Seraglio the boys were shut off from the outside world and lived in a competitive atmosphere, vying with each other to gain the highest places. Any office in the state, save only that of Sultan, was open to them if they worked hard, and they responded to the challenge with great dedication.

When their training was complete they were appointed to posts in the army and civil service according to their particular talents. To all intents and purposes they had become nobles—yet they remained the Sultan's slaves to the end. Unlike Plato's guardians, they were allowed to gather wealth and start families, and it was here that the system broke down. Naturally those who had passed through the Grand Seraglio wanted to 'send their sons to the old school', and finally they were allowed in, followed by the sons of free-born Turks. The system could not retain its original character once it ceased to recruit solely from first generation slaves.

Plato's writings were known in Muslim lands at the time of Muhammed the Conqueror, but there is no evidence of whether the Grand Seraglio was directly modelled on *The Republic*. In any case, Plato would have given the project but half-hearted support, because he would have disapproved of appointing slaves to high office. He assumed that guardians would be drawn from the best families in the land, and the qualities which he looked for in his ideal man were essentially those of an aristocrat.

The Platonist ideal exercised a more lasting influence over the development of public school education in England in

from Spy cartoons:
*Some Victorian
Schoolmasters*

the nineteenth century. Society was undergoing rapid upheaval. A class of men had arisen who had prospered from the Industrial Revolution. The first generations of these 'new rich' were homespun characters with provincial accents, and when they found themselves shut out of fashionable society, they looked for schools which would provide their sons with the social polish that they themselves lacked.

Around the middle of the century the public school system began to expand to meet this new demand. Matthew Arnold, son of the great headmaster, declared:

> It is only in England that this beneficial salutary inter-mixture of classes takes place. Look at the bottle-merchant's son, and the Plantagenet being brought up side by side. None of your absurd separations and quarterings here. Very likely young Bottles will end up by being a lord himself.

Like the Grand Seraglio, the public schools were expressly designed for training up a ruling élite. Whether Muhammed the Conqueror knew his Plato or not, Samuel Butler of Shrewsbury, Thomas Arnold of Rugby and the other great headmasters of the century certainly did. Plato's system, of course, needed modifications. No one was bold enough to propose that the class which had profited

from the Industrial Revolution should be separated from its wealth. Moreover, the idea of holding wives in common would scarcely have gained favour in Victorian England. Ideals of character training, however, closely followed Plato's model.

The public school ethos was largely an extension of the beliefs and personality of a single man, Thomas Arnold, who became headmaster of Rugby in 1828. Before that date the ancient schools had been passing through evil days. The Rev. John Bowdler, who later put his name into the English language by producing purged editions of Shakespeare's plays, complained that:

public schools are the seats and nurseries of vice. It may be un-avoidable, or it may be not, but the fact is indisputable. None can pass through a large school without being pretty intimately acquainted with vice; and few, alas! very few, without tasting too largely of that poisoned bowl.

No one reading Thomas Hughes' *Tom Brown's Schooldays* could assert that this was simply the judgement of an over-sensitive Victorian cleric. The schools were places where, in Arnold's words, a boy 'loses his modesty, his respect for the truth, and his affectionateness, and becomes coarse, and false, and unfeeling'.

Arnold accepted the post at Rugby only on condition that he should be granted absolute power to carry out his reforms, and he achieved his object by free use of the twin sanctions of expulsion and corporal punishment. Evil elements within the school society had to be cut out without compunction.

Till a man learns that the first, second and third duty of a schoolmaster is to get rid of unpromising subjects, a great public school will never be what it might be and what it ought to be.

Arnold certainly practised what he preached. A boy in the upper school could expect to be expelled instantly for lying and many other crimes. Sometimes Arnold would expel whole groups of boys together. After one such incident he stood in front of the discontented pupils and declared:

It is *not* necessary that this should be a school of three hundred, or one hundred, or of fifty boys: but it *is* necessary that it should be a school of Christian gentlemen.

Parents complained that he used his powers capriciously, keeping one boy after a major offence yet asking another to leave after a small one. The headmaster, however, would not even discuss his powers; he was the sole judge of whether a boy was suited to stay at the school.

Flogging had always been an integral part of the public school system, and Arnold saw no cause to do away with it. It was, he declared, 'fitly answering to and marking the naturally inferior state of boyhood, and therefore conveyed no particular degradation to persons in such a state'. He defended the right of older pupils to chastise the younger on the grounds that it was preparing them to exercise power in later life. His sixth formers were to be like officers in the armed forces, from whom a refusal to punish would be interpreted as a lack of moral fibre. Once again the issue was above discussion.

I do not choose to discuss the thickness of Praepostors' sticks, or the greater or less blackness of a boy's bruises, for the amusement of all the readers of the newspapers.

These negative aspects of Arnold's regime at Rugby were only a means of achieving a greater end. His whole educational programme was devised to turn out young men who would merit the description constantly upon his lips—'a Christian and a gentleman'. The chapel was the heart of the school, and week after week the boys listened as the doctor expounded the duties and the responsibilities of a leader.

Is it possible for anyone who believes what Christ has said, to rest contented, either for himself or for others, with that very low and very unchristian standard which he sees and knows to prevail generally in the world? Is it possible for him not to wish, for himself and for all in whose welfare he is interested, that they may belong to the small minority in matters of principle and practice, rather than to the large majority.

Arnold's powerful personality transformed Rugby into a community, moulded after his own image. He also won over both pupils and members of his staff as lifelong devotees of his methods. When there was a vacancy for a head in another public school, the governors generally turned to Arnold for advice as to who would be the best candidate for the post. Within one generation the Arnold tradition had been firmly emplanted in the public school system. In chapel and classroom, from masters and prefects, pupils up and down the country learned the same lesson. Public school boys belonged to a privileged class, and privilege carried responsibilities. They would never be their own men, for they represented a nation and a way of life; in Newbolt's words, 'what you are the race shall be'.

Within the limits of what they set out to achieve, the best of the English public schools provided education of a very high order. Whether the ultimate balance of account is in credit or debit remains a matter of social values. Boys who spent their formative years cut off from society too often became insensitive to other people's lives and emotions. Even when they moved to distant parts of the Empire, they had an uncanny knack of recreating the élitist society in which they had been nurtured. On the credit side, the future rulers of the short-lived British Empire did generally learn their lesson of *noblesse oblige,* and possessed an integrity which had been generally lacking among earlier generations of Empire builders.

The second half of the twentieth century has witnessed the rapid disintegration of this Empire, but the public

Eton College

schools continue to exercise a powerful influence on British life. Analysis of the educational background of those holding influential posts in industry, commerce, politics, science, education and the Church shows that a large proportion still start with a public school training. Some of these schools cling tenaciously to old ways represented by institutions such as fagging and flogging. Many, however, have adapted their methods to the changing needs of the twentieth century.

It is widely recognized, both within the public schools and without, that it is necessary to break the élitist image. 'Young Bottles' may have had his place at Rugby, but his father had to make a fortune first, and a modern public school education is far beyond the means of a worker or lower-paid professional man. The Newsom Commission, charged to find ways of bringing these schools within the state system, saw three alternative methods of tackling the question. Each, however, raised serious problems.

In the first place local authorities could give grants to

pay the fees of pupils who would benefit from a public school education. Teachers in the state system naturally object to the idea that their most able pupils should be channelled off, and argue that any kind of scholarship system would only prolong the public schools' grip on British education. Teachers in public schools, no less naturally, object to the idea that suitability for boarding education should be interpreted to include only those who have no stable home background, thus compelling their schools to absorb a large number of disturbed, and not necessarily able, pupils.

The second proposal was that the public schools should be abolished altogether, and all education be brought within the state system. Opponents protest that this very drastic solution would involve the destruction of many excellent schools, and would take away parents' right of choice in a free society.

The third possibility would be to do nothing either to help or to harm the public schools. It is argued that in time parents would see that they did not need to buy opportunities for their children, but would willingly entrust them to the state system. Opponents argue that this course of inaction would do nothing to break up the inequalities of Britain's class-bound society.

The choice is essentially a political one, and must therefore ultimately lie with legislators rather than teachers. The issue is not a simple judgement on particular schools, or the general desirability of boarding education. It involves a fundamental reassessment of whether a Platonic education, reserved for the potential leaders, has any relevance to the needs of an advanced modern society.

4. Teaching the Believer

I went to a teacher, teacher, teacher,
I went to a teacher to save my soul;
Teacher was a preacher, preacher, preacher,
Teacher was a preacher so I was told.

I learnt my lesson, lesson, lesson,
I learnt my lesson to save my soul;
Wasn't it a blessin', blessin', blessin',
Wasn't that a blessin' so I was told.

HUDDIE LEDBETTER.

Plato understood better than any of his contemporaries that education in its fullest sense is not simply a process of inculcating a child with military prowess or scribal techniques. It is the method by which a whole pattern of culture is passed from one generation to the next. Different societies adopt beliefs and formulate codes of behaviour which provide a framework for social intercourse. In time these crystallize into some form of religion.

In India education developed early along religious lines. It did not aim primarily at producing warriors, as in the West, or scribes, as in China, but was a means of initiating the Brahmin caste into the mysteries of their religious cults. The priest had his own specialized functions within society; if he neglected them the whole pattern of conception and birth, life and harvest, were brought into jeopardy. A vast number of hymns and prayers became associated with varied religious rites, and every one of these had to be committed to memory. One pupil, for instance, might be expected to learn the ancient collection of 1,017 hymns called the *Rigveda*. A teacher would chant the verse of a hymn and the children would repeat it after him until they were all word perfect. Then they would move on to the next verse. Everything depended on complete accuracy, for a

33

single slip in the intonation of a word could destroy the power of the whole religious action. Under this training children performed immense feats of memory. In time the language became obsolete and neither teacher nor pupil understood what he was saying, but the hymns were still passed down the generations with complete accuracy.

Similar religious schools exist today in the more remote Muslim areas of the world. Boys are to be seen sitting by the roadside, rocking on their haunches as they chant passages from the Koran over and over again. They are speaking in classical Arabic, which they probably do not understand, but the virtue of the exercise lies not in *understanding* but in *possessing* the sacred texts.

Another part of the Eastern tradition, however, does stress understanding in a way that is proving attractive to modern man. The Buddha taught that the ultimate aim of human life is to reach such a depth of knowledge that the individual loses all sense of his own personality in the

Algeria: a class in the Koran for students of all ages

vastness of the universe. Such 'mysticism' cannot be learned by chanting religious hymns, but is rather a state of mind achieved through contemplation. Buddhist students attach themselves to wandering teachers, and under their guidance seek to rise to the state of perfection.

The Jewish culture also produced an educational system which was religious in aims and content. Like the Hindus, the Jews had sacred texts which had to be learned by heart. The most important of these was the Pentateuch—the five books of the law. Jewish daily life was governed by a multitude of religious rules and regulations, and anyone who was ignorant of the law lived in danger of committing an offence at almost every turn in his life. The child was also instructed in the history of his race. The Jewish people had been chosen by God, and history was the record of a special relationship with him.

Only take heed, and keep your soul diligently, lest you forget the things which your eyes have seen, and lest they depart from your heart all the days of your life; make them known to your children and your children's children—how on the day that you stood before the Lord your God at Horeb, the Lord said to me, 'Gather the people to me, that I may let them hear my words, so that they may learn to fear me all the days that they live on the earth, and that they may teach their children so!'

The Jews would never have considered delegating this responsible task to the riff-raff of society, as did the Greeks. In Old Testament times the father of the family was responsible for his children's education, but nearer the time of Christ the law became so complicated that instruction was handed over to specialists. The teacher was the most honoured man in society, and the schoolroom was more sacred than the synagogue itself.

This tradition was inherited by the Christian Church. The early Christians would not allow their children to attend the classical schools for fear that they would be corrupted by pagan teachers and immoral classical texts. As Christianity spread through the ancient world, however, believers found it impossible to segregate their children, so they sent them to school armed with a warning to 'keep the passions of Homer at arm's length'.

Sabbath Eve at an Israeli Youth Village

When Christianity became the official religion of the Roman Empire the classical and the religious traditions of education merged into one, and out of their marriage was born the educational system that was to hold sway in the West until modern times. From Greece and Rome came the grounding of education in classical studies; from Judaism came the link between teaching and a moral training.

For a time, as the barbarians plundered the Roman Empire, it appeared that education and civilization had perished together. But the classical/Christian tradition survived precariously within the monasteries, and, when rulers like Charlemagne and Alfred the Great wanted to revive studies among their people, they turned to the monks for help.

For the thousand years between 500 and 1500 A.D., literacy was virtually a monopoly of the Church. When St Patrick had a young man sent to him to train as a monk, he first baptised him and then gave him a copy of the alphabet. The monastic schools were founded with the specific purpose of training novices, but they provided some sort of educational service for the wider community. Sometimes the teaching was ill-suited to the needs of a layman's son. In the sixteenth century Erasmus complained that boys were kept in monasteries:

solely and simply to sing hymns to the Virgin; they do not understand what they are singing, yet according to the priests it con-
stitutes the whole of religion. Money must be raised to buy organs
and train boys to squeal and to learn no other thing that is good
for them.

Such a condemnation was often justified. Most of the
schools were tiny and many were inefficient. It has been
estimated, however, that in the late middle ages there was
one grammar school for every 5,625 of the population, while
in 1864 the proportion had dropped to one for every 23,750.
Beyond this, a great many children were taught some rudiments of knowledge by their local parish priests.

Medieval education was based entirely on the concept of
authority. Learning had slipped back a long way since classical times, and emphasis was placed on making good the
loss rather than on breaking new ground. Teachers assumed
that all wisdom and all knowledge were to be found in the
old writings. On the one hand was the Bible and the early
fathers of the Church; on the other hand were the old
classical writers, and especially Aristotle, the most famous
pupil of Plato's Academy. If a medieval scholar wanted to
examine any matter he would follow a set routine. He would
first study the Bible to see if there was any clear text which

An outer monastic school in the middle ages

would settle the issue beyond doubt. Failing that, he would dig his way through the ancient authors and line up all the opinions on each side. The matter would be decided by the weight of opinion on both sides. This method applied, not only in matters of opinion, but to matters of fact, which the scholar could quite easily have gone out and checked with his own eyes. To the medieval teacher, truth lay between the covers of a book, and not in man's reasoning powers. That was why the monks spent such endless hours copying out the texts of the old writings in the cloisters of their monasteries. The main function of education was to teach obedience.

The Renaissance did not change this outlook as much as has been commonly supposed. What happened was that, with the discovery of the pure texts, like Poggio's Quintilian, the emphasis shifted from the religious to the classical authorities. It was a rediscovery of past treasures, rather than an awakening of man's reasoning powers.

> I affirm (wrote Erasmus) that with slight qualification the whole of attainable knowledge lies enclosed within the literary monuments of ancient Greece.

During the Renaissance education began to break out of the control of the Church. The change can be best illustrated from the foundation of two English public schools—Winchester in the fourteenth century, and St Paul's at the beginning of the sixteenth. The first was a typical monastic school. Pupils had to wear the tonsure like monks and were intended for the priesthood. The aim of the school was 'that Christ may be more fervently and frequently preached, and faith and the worship of God's name increased and more firmly maintained'.

John Colet, the founder of St Paul's, was himself a clergyman, and his school was also Christian in character. The novelty was that he cut its links with the Church as an institution, and put it under the control of a London trading company. He intended that 'real Christian principles' should be combined with sound classical learning in his school. His friend Erasmus helped to arrange the course of studies, and Dr Lily, the first High Master, wrote a Latin grammar, which was destined to be the standard text book for centuries to come.

Many schools were founded, or refounded, after the pattern of St Paul's, but, even as Colet and Erasmus were working on their new school, the Reformation was beginning, and this was destined to put the religious issue right back into the heart of education. Within a few years Western Europe was split into two bitterly hostile camps. Neither Protestant nor Catholic could afford to neglect the schoolroom, and a battle was joined for the minds of succeeding generations. The most systematic exponent on the Protestant side was John Calvin, and on the Catholic side Ignatius Loyola, founder of the Jesuits.

The two men had much in common. Both looked on the young mind as 'soft wax' which had to be moulded by relentless discipline; both emphasized that the task of teaching could only be undertaken by men of the highest ability and integrity.

Loyola, himself of noble stock, insisted that no man should be too proud to be a teacher. The pupils for his schools were drawn from the ranks of the well-born and the able, because he believed that, if Catholicism was to command the allegiance of a people, it must first command the allegiance of its natural leaders. The boys who came out of his schools lived up to his expectations, and the Jesuit movement was largely responsible for stemming the tide of Protestantism.

Calvin's influence can best be seen in the work of his disciple John Knox, in Scotland. He had a profound respect for education, and believed that it should be broadly based in the humble people of the land. From his time onwards teachers and learning gained a respect in that country which they never achieved south of the border. Even poor parents hoped that their sons would prove themselves fit to go on to the university and become ministers in the Kirk. At the beginning of term boys would set out from their humble crofts with bags of meal slung over their shoulders and tramp across the countryside towards centres like St Andrews or Glasgow. Children and parents alike made sacrifices in the cause of learning which were unheard of in England.

Both Loyola and Calvin based their teaching programmes

on the doctrine of original sin. Man was born 'in sin', with a natural tendency towards evil. The educational process was designed to check the child's natural instincts and direct him on the narrow path of virtue. Under both systems the schoolmaster was a stern and remote figure, not especially brutal by the standards of the day, but prepared to use any means, including fear of hell fire, to conquer the evil in human nature. James Joyce in *A Portrait of the Artist as a Young Man* gives a vivid account of the effects of a sermon, which could just as well have come from a Calvinist pulpit.

John Wesley, the eighteenth century founder of Methodism, did not accept this harsh doctrine. He believed that man was not born in sin, but became sinful through contact with the world, and he founded a school for the sons of his preachers where everything possible would be done to prevent the contagion of sin from ever creeping into their lives. The children were to come when they were only five years old and stay for at least ten years, without ever going on holiday. Their day was filled with study and worship, leaving no time for play, when they might be expected to get into mischief. They were never to be allowed out of sight of the staff, and were even to sleep under supervision, with a light burning in their dormitory.

Wesley's experiment was mercifully short-lived. He explained its failure by the fact that none of the masters he appointed had been brought up under a similar routine, so were themselves tainted with sin and unfit to run the school. Despite this failure, however, Wesley was to have an immense influence on the history of education.

He spent his long life carrying the gospel to the common man. Crowds came to hear him preach, and he built up a substantial following. His disciple Francis Asbury preached the same message across America, and a great religious movement started on both sides of the Atlantic. This set up a reaction within the established Church, and once again the Churches were in bitter competition, each trying to build up a following.

The task of teaching all adults to read was clearly too great, but at least an attempt could be made to enlighten the young. Since most children worked for six days in the week, they could only be reached through Sunday schools.

As a result, children who spent all week in a factory began to spend their Sundays spelling out the alphabet, singing hymns and committing chunks of the Bible to memory. It was clearly an unsatisfactory solution, and, when Acts were passed limiting child labour, the religious organizations were able to turn their Sunday schools into normal day schools.

If the Churches can claim credit for giving the initial impetus to popular education in England, they must also bear responsibility for holding back its wider development during the nineteenth century, when they had not the financial resources to provide schooling for every child. The state began to contribute money to the religious societies in 1833, but even with this help they could not meet the needs of the rising population. Yet every time politicians suggested that the state should take direct responsibility for schooling, they were met with a seemingly insoluble problem. Anglicans argued that state schools should teach only the religion of the established Church. Nonconformists replied that they would rather go to prison than pay rates to support Anglican schools.

A compromise was at last reached in 1870 when Anglicans grudgingly conceded that the religious instruction in state schools should be of a 'non-denominational' variety. This broad agreement established the guidelines for development in the past century. English schoolchildren still begin the day with a religious assembly and have one period of religious instruction a week, when—officially at any rate—they are taught from a syllabus agreed by members of different Churches.

In the United States the problem was still further complicated by the presence of large Jewish and other non-Christian minorities in some states. Politicians on both sides of the Atlantic show a natural reluctance to grasp the nettle of religious controversy, and the matter was decided by recourse to the courts. By a Supreme Court judgement of 1948, religion was excluded from the syllabus in all state schools.

It is now widely accepted, by Christians and non-Christians alike, that the assumptions on which medieval education was constructed are no longer tenable. The arrival

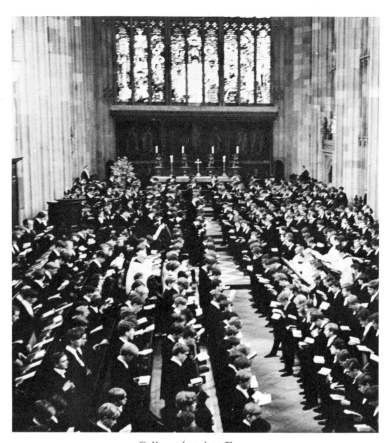

College chapel at Eton

of science in the curriculum has cast doubts on traditional concepts of authority, and the study of child psychology has rocked the doctrine of original sin. Men ask whether the teaching of virtue should be linked with religious statements which are no longer universally accepted as true. Bertrand Russell expressed the humanist point of view.

How can you teach them to be good if you habitually and deliberately lie to them on a subject of the greatest importance? And how can any conduct which is genuinely desirable need false beliefs as its motive? If there are no valid arguments for what you consider 'good' conduct, your concept of goodness must be at fault.

Defenders of religious education argue that humanists like

Russell are living on borrowed Christian virtues which might survive a couple of generations when cut off from their source but no more.

It is broadly true to say that the Protestant Churches have accepted a pattern of change, and handed education over to the state. They hope that teachers of their own persuasion will influence the rising generation, but they have given up the attempt to run the system. The Roman Church, however, holds to the principle that a Catholic child should be taught in a Catholic school. In response to the accusation that this is a blatant 'conditioning' process, Church leaders argue, as Loyola had done, that children must be brought up within the faith, and conditioning is an essential part of learning.

It is impossible to make a simple judgement on the influence of religion. It has provided the impetus behind movements for popular education and has done much to improve the status of the teacher. On the other hand it has introduced an unhealthy emphasis on guilt and it has entangled schooling systems in religious quarrels—often to their incalculable harm. But, whether for good or ill, religion has played a decisive role in the story of teaching.

5. Teaching the Scientist

They equate the home of the human race to a wandering star.
They pack men, animals, plants, and the earth itself onto a cart
and trundle it in a circle through an empty sky. There is no longer
any difference between the Upper and the Lower, between the
Eternal and the Temporal. That we pass away, we know. That
heaven too passes away, they now inform us.

VERY THIN MONK
BERTHOLD BRECHT's *Galileo*

WE have seen that Renaissance scholars did not
break suddenly with old ideas of authority. Erasmus
could declare that all wisdom lay in the writings of
ancient Greece, but in fact by his time man had just about
made good the deficit of the dark ages. If any progress was
to be made scholars had to put down their old books and
discover new worlds for themselves. This is the major
watershed of the history of education. Teaching may be
classified as 'ancient' or 'modern' according to whether it
encourages respect for authorities, which cannot be questioned, or challenges the pupils to find answers to problems
for themselves, using their own senses to conduct experiments.

The thirteenth century friar Roger Bacon could, by this
definition, lay claim to being the first of the moderns. He
protested vigorously against the endless study of old authors
which passed for education in his day. Were the fathers not
human beings like anyone else, he argued; was not man still
endowed with the same faculties as in ancient times? True
knowledge was not delivered by authority but grew out of
experience.

If any man who had never seen fire were to prove by satisfactory
argument that fire burns and destroys things, the hearer's mind
would not be satisfied, nor would he avoid fire until by putting his
hand or some combustible thing into it, he proved by actual
experiment what the argument laid down.

44

If Roger Bacon had been born in another age he might have been one of the world's great scientists, but his was a lone voice and he could not break the established patterns.

Bacon would not have accepted that there was any conflict between science and religion. Since the world belonged to God, experiment and observation were simply methods of discovering more about creation. Science had, indeed, been born as a handmaid of religion. Priests who wanted to calculate the movements of the sun and planets for religious festivals learned to use surprisingly complex mathematical calculations. Since the stars were the source of power, mathematics was closely linked with astronomy. 'Wise men' tried to discover patterns and 'emanations' of heavenly bodies which influenced men's lives, so that the magician and astrologer were forerunners of the modern scientist.

The Greeks developed mathematics to a high level, and Plato expected his guardians to spend ten years, from the time they were twenty, in its study. Plato favoured mathematics because it was purely abstract. It had no direct contact with the world of objects and living creatures, but trained the mind in preparation for the study of philosophy. In contrast, subjects like medicine and engineering were beneath the attention of a leader of society. In this Plato was at one with his contemporaries. Important scientific work was done in classical times, but this was the work of a few specialists and was separated from the main stream of education. Medieval teachers accepted this tradition uncritically.

In the sixteenth century man's horizons were suddenly pushed further outwards, and fresh fields for study were uncovered. The opening of ocean trade routes and the discovery of the New World aroused interest in maps and navigational instruments; the invention of printing had made it possible for new ideas to spread much more rapidly than in the past. The Arabic method of numbering had at last established itself in common use. Scientific studies could not develop far as long as men were condemned to writing a simple number like 1,837 as LMCCCXXXVII! Galileo, the greatest of a new generation of scientists, used the telescope to prove that the earth moved round the sun. A crisis in

human thought had arrived. The authorities—both Christian and classical—declared that the earth was stationary,
and the Church predictably pronounced against the
scientist. It is easy for modern men to mock a seventeenth
century pope for being reactionary, but patterns of thinking
established over thousands of years could not change
overnight.

The new sciences were able to develop more freely in
Protestant countries, and a keen interest arose among
members of the English middle class. The King and leaders
of the Church disapproved of the new trends. An arch-
deacon poured scorn on people who preferred reason and
experiment before the literal words of the Scripture;
arguments in favour of Galileo's theory, he declared, 'may
go current in a mechanical tradesman's shop, yet are very
insufficient to be allowed for good by men of learning and
Christians by profession'.

It was natural that the 'mechanics' should begin to look
for an educational system which would take account of the
new developments in science, and in 1598 Gresham's
College was founded to meet this demand. Physics, geometry and astronomy were included in the syllabus and
for the first time logarithms were brought into use as an aid
to teaching mathematics.

The chief spokesman of the new movement was by
coincidence another Bacon—Francis Bacon, Chancellor of
England. He declared that up to his day man had been in a
state of childhood, having to be protected by his authorities,
but the time had come to 'hand over to men their fortunes,
the understanding having been emancipated—having come,
so to speak, of age'.

The universities and old established schools, however,
refused to be shaken out of their traditional ways. Educators
sneered at the new studies as 'the business of traders,
merchants, seamen, carpenters, surveyors of lands and the
like; and perhaps some almanac makers in London'. Most
schoolboys could still expect to spend their time in the study
of rhetoric and in endless hours of Latin and Greek.

By 1640 England was deeply divided on matters of religion
and government, and the party which opposed the King
in political matters also took up the cause of educational

reform. In 1641, on the eve of the outbreak of war, Parliament took the remarkable step of inviting a well-known
Czech called Comenius to come to England to advise on
educational matters.

At first sight Comenius might seem a somewhat im-
probable warrior in the cause of the scientific method. He
was a bishop of the Moravian Church, but had been forced
into exile when his native Bohemia was captured by Catholic
troops in the Thirty Years War. His religious views would
today be classified as 'fundamentalist'. Like many of his
contemporaries he thought that the time had almost come
for Christ to return and set up God's kingdom on earth.

He had spent many years of his exile working as a teacher,
and during that time had become interested in Francis
Bacon's new science. He did not recognize that there could
be any conflict between the truths of science and the truths
of religion. Indeed, it seemed to him that if the new science
could only be joined to the old faith, superstition and ignorance would be finally swept away, and there would be
nothing to hinder the great day of Christ's coming.

To Comenius, therefore, education was more than a means
of training the young; it was the very agent by which the
kingdom of God would be ushered in. He was a bitter critic
of traditional schools, which he described as 'slaughter
houses of the young', and proposed a new kind of education
in which all the senses would join in the excitement of
discovery. The golden rule for teachers was that:

everything should, as far as possible, be placed before the senses.
Everything visible should be brought before the organ of sight,
everything audible before that of hearing. Odours should be placed
before the sense of smell, and the things that are tastable and
tangible before the sense of taste and touch respectively.

For this there are three cogent reasons. Firstly, the commence-
ment of knowledge must always come from the senses (for the
understanding possesses nothing that it has not derived from the
senses). Surely, then, the beginning of wisdom should consist, not
in the mere learning the names of things, but in the actual perception of the things themselves! It is when the thing has been
grasped by the senses that language should fulfil its function of
explaining it still further.

Secondly, the truth and certainty of science depend more on the witness of the senses than on anything else . . .

Thirdly, since the senses are the most trusty servants of the memory, this method of sensuous perception, if universally applied, will lead to the permanent retention of knowledge that has once been acquired.

Comenius' visit was, however, cut short by the outbreak of war between King and Parliament, and his supporters had to abandon the realm of ideas and take to the battlefield. When Parliament emerged victorious it appeared that the opportunity had come at last for a radical overhaul of the old educational system. The country squires and 'mechanics' who now ruled England wanted schools to teach modern subjects which would be directly useful to their sons in future life. Oxford and Cambridge were too set in their ways to change, but a short-lived university for the north country was founded in Durham and plans were made for a similar foundation in London. Existing schools were brought under strict supervision, and there were those who looked for the day when every child in England would go to school.

But high ideals could not run a country, and the experiment of the Commonwealth failed. The new king, Charles II, took a personal interest in science, and some of the dons at Oxford and Cambridge were becoming involved in interesting experiments. On the institutional level, however, the old pattern was restored intact. The Restoration was a victory for the old way of life. Durham University was closed and school teachers returned dutifully—and perhaps thankfully—to the time-honoured methods.

Meanwhile the new studies were making better progress on the Continent. The Jesuits introduced physics into their academies in the belief that it 'disposed the mind to theology'. In 1642 a regulation was set down in the German state of Saxe-Coburg-Gotha, making science teaching compulsory in state schools. In England, however, education retreated into a classicism from which all meaning, all life had gone. 'Classical education is absolutely necessary for everybody,' declared Lord Chesterfield, 'because everybody has agreed to call it so.' By the eighteenth century ancient grammar and public schools had lapsed into mere parodies of their former standards. 'Young gentlemen themselves so frequently hear the learning which is taught in schools and universities ridiculed, that they often make themselves easy with giving a very superficial attention to it.'

The eighteenth century saw the birth of the Industrial Revolution. But, though it was born on English soil, the English educational system can scarcely claim any part in its early achievements. The great engineers, inventors and industrialists were drawn almost to a man from outside the privileged classes. Some were Scotsmen; some were nonconformists who had been excluded from traditional schooling; some were even illiterates who had to master their skills the hard way.

The only schools which could claim any credit for the achievements of the Industrial Revolution were a handful of dissenting academies set up by nonconformist ministers who had been driven out of the Church of England. In the early days these schools faced considerable persecution—they could not be established within five miles of a chartered town, and in some cases master and pupils had to move from place to place to avoid the attentions of hostile authorities. But they managed to survive, and maintained a high level of scientific education. One of the earliest of the academies was at Newington Green near London, where Charles Morton set up a laboratory which contained 'some not inconsiderable rarities with air pump, thermometer, and all sorts of mathematical instruments'. A century later the famous chemist Joseph Priestley was a teacher in the academy at Warrington.

Many famous people were educated in these schools, and some went on to follow courses in a Scottish university, since Oxford and Cambridge were closed to dissenters. These academies had considerable influence on the development of education on the other side of the Atlantic. Many of the New England settlers were descended from the parliamentarians who had invited Comenius to England. Charles Morton of Newington Green must, therefore, have felt that he was among friends when he went to Massachusetts, eventually becoming vice-president of Harvard. During his period of office there he helped to establish scientific education in the young college on a firm footing. When Joseph Priestley's house in Birmingham was burnt by an angry mob a century later, he likewise took refuge in the friendly atmosphere of America, where he was formally welcomed by the first association of American teachers.

The thirteen colonies had inherited a pattern of classical schools from the mother country, but the inhabitants of a new land were eager to find a more practical basis for education. In 1743 Benjamin Franklin proposed that English should replace classics as the focus of instruction and that natural sciences should be established in the syllabus. He was not immediately successful, and, when the first of the American academies was opened in Philadelphia six years later, it was still a classical school. It was not long, however, before Franklin's ideas prevailed, and a bias towards scientific and practical studies became the norm of American education.

Similar progress was being made in Prussia in the early nineteenth century, and soon England, which at one time had been in the vanguard of the new education, was the main stronghold of the old disciplines. All the headmasters of the revived public schools were classicists. Butler's successor at Shrewsbury was Kennedy, whose Latin grammar replaced Lily's as the standard work and held the field well into the twentieth century. Kennedy insisted that the sciences did not furnish a basis for education. Although classics had no immediate application to life, he argued, they provided a mental discipline which could be transferred into any field of endeavour. The opposite point of view was powerfully presented by Herbert Spencer, who poured scorn on the failure of teachers to prepare children to live in the contemporary world.

Men who would blush if caught saying Iphigénia instead of Iphigenía, or who would resent as an insult any imputation of ignorance respecting the fabled labours of a demi-god, show not the slightest shame in confessing that they do not know where the Eustachian tubes are, what are the actions of the spinal cord, what is the normal rate of pulsation, or how the lungs are inflated.

He argued that a study of science not only prepared a child to meet the practical challenges of life, but also presented a vision of beauty and provided an excellent all-round mental discipline.

Early nineteenth-century chemistry laboratory

In the middle years of the nineteenth century the new disciplines began to challenge traditional religion as well as the classics. Students of geology had discovered fossils in rocks which appeared to prove that the world was much older than the traditional calculation, based on the book of Genesis, would allow. The publication of Darwin's *Origin of Species* in 1859 caused a public scandal. Christians were again faced with a painful reassessment of fundamental principles and, once again, a 'flat earth brigade' failed to make the adjustment. Small groups of fanatics fought to keep new knowledge about the origins of the world and man out of the schools, but they had little success outside the 'Bible belt' of the American South.

As late as 1925 the Tennessee state legislature over-whelmingly passed a law banning the teaching of evolution in all state schools. John T. Stopes, biology teacher at Dayton, chose to defy the law, and, after one of the most remarkable trials in modern history, he was convicted. Several states passed similar laws, and, though rarely enforced, they remained on the statute books until 1968, when the Supreme Court ruled that they were an infringement of liberty and so unconstitutional.

In the twentieth century the demands of industry on the educational system were growing daily. It was impossible for teachers to argue that 'practical' subjects had no place on the time-table. By 1900 the two countries with the most advanced technical and scientific schools—Germany and the United States—had pushed their industrial production well beyond Britain's. When the Japanese decided to enter the industrial race they surveyed European education, decided that the German pattern was most likely to bring them success in their efforts and faithfully copied it in all details.

Even those last bastions of the classical pattern, the English public schools, have finally adjusted the emphasis of their teaching. Latin and Greek have become two subjects among many, competing for space on an overcrowded time-table. Few would deny that classical literature is too rich to be jettisoned from the educational process, but it is open to debate whether the study of dead languages should not be confined to the realm of higher education.

After three hundred years, the change in emphasis which Comenius looked for has been accomplished. Governments pour their wealth into technical and scientific training

Chemistry laboratory at a girls' grammar school

because national survival depends upon it. Russian achievements in space technology have spurred the American government on to a vast expansion in scientific and technical education. The schoolroom has become a major factor in international rivalry. Pupils are faced with new knowledge which increases in sheer bulk year by year. The old Platonic ideal of leisurely education, far removed from the trivial preoccupations of everyday life, has been swept away by events. University expansion is planned in relationship to the demands of a technological society. In Britain two thirds of all the places in institutions of higher education are set aside for students of pure and applied science.

The pupils themselves, however, refuse to conform to the pattern laid down for them. Arnold Toynbee has predicted that the next generation will swing away from technology. Certainly half of Britain's sixth-formers stubbornly present themselves for university training in the arts subjects. In the age of the atomic bomb there may be an increasing number who share the fear of the Very Thin Monk that science will take man too far.

We shall live to see the day when they will say; there are no longer men and animals, man is an animal, there is nothing but animals.

The establishment of practical subjects in the school curriculum has not achieved all that Herbert Spencer predicted. In a number of American high schools subjects like cookery and handicrafts—worthy in themselves—have become something of a cuckoo in the nest, elbowing more 'academic' studies from their rightful place on the time-table. It is also possible for practical subjects to become as formalized and sterile as the older disciplines, and a fair amount of science teaching can only be classified as ancient by our earlier definition. But it is at last becoming recognized that the old disputes are barren. Education is now a practical preparation for a highly complex world; at the same time teachers do not have to justify every piece of study on the basis of 'practical application'. Left to themselves children have known all the time that the whole environment of their lives is worthy of exploration—just because it is interesting.

6. Teaching the Worker

Even if it were possible, I doubt whether it would be desirable, with a view to the real interests of the peasant boy, to keep him at school till he was fourteen or fifteen years of age. But it is not possible. We must make up our minds to see the last of him, as far as the day school is concerned, at ten or eleven. We must frame our system of education on this hypothesis; and I venture to maintain that it is quite possible to teach a child soundly and thoroughly, in a way that he shall not forget it, all that is necessary for him to possess in the shape of intellectual attainment, by the time that he is ten years old.

THE REV. J. FRASER (LATER BISHOP OF MANCHESTER), 1861

UNTIL quite recent times the vast proportion of mankind has received no formal education at all. The nineteenth century clergyman's contemptuous dismissal of higher education for the 'peasants' sounds highly offensive to the modern ear, but only a century before his time schooling even up to the age of ten was a rare privilege.

The future bishop was using the word 'peasants' interchangeably with 'lower classes', but it is important to draw a distinction between the country farmer and the town worker. In 1700 Britain, in common with the rest of Europe, could properly be called a peasant community. Eight out of ten people lived in villages and grew food for their own families, producing just a small surplus to sell to town dwellers. Peasant communities of this sort are universally ill-educated, and a large proportion of such subsistence farmers in the world today are still illiterate.

Within the towns, however, there grew up another branch of the 'lower classes'. Many of these possessed specialised skills which they practised for a living. These were not taught in schoolrooms, but were handed down from one generation to the next by the apprenticeship system.

Youngsters learned their trade first by watching their masters, then by handling the tools and materials for themselves.

The sixteenth century reformers first introduced the idea that book learning was desirable for men who worked with their hands. Martin Luther translated the Bible into German and William Tyndale translated it into English. Copies of these vernacular scriptures were then prominently displayed in churches where simple ploughboys and apprentices would be able to come and study them at leisure. The only problem was that neither the ploughboy nor the apprentice could read. Wealthy men, who in the middle ages would have left their money to monasteries, now founded charity schools, like Christ's Hospital, where deserving poor children would receive the benefits of education. When religious fervour waned in the eighteenth century, however, most of these charity schools either fell onto evil days, or were usurped for the use of higher-born children. By 1800 it was still the case that the majority of the poor people of England could neither read nor write.

North of the border, however, the picture was very different. The Scots had good cause to be proud of their schools, and could boast that 'scarcely a single individual of mature age could be found in the lowland parishes who was unable to read'. The Scottish system of education grew straight from the Calvinist root. Since a man or woman's status was measured by his standing in the eyes of God, birth and breeding counted for less than they did south of the border.

Every parish had its own school, under the care of a master, who had generally graduated from one of the five universities. He was appointed by the kirk session, and could be dismissed if he failed to live up to the standard expected of his calling. Thus one Robert Inglis was dismissed 'for drunkenness and scandalous carriage with Elspeth Morrison', and Hugh Mair, more surprisingly, 'for exercising too rigid and cruel discipline'.

Although Scottish teachers were expected to be learned and upright their rewards were meagre. Many were forced to carry on some trade in their spare time—and they had little enough of that. Some were even reduced to organizing

E

cock-fighting to keep themselves and their families alive. Many of their pupils trudged miles to be in school by 7 o'clock in the morning. The whole educational process was single-minded and purposeful. In the early days some kirk sessions went as far as to abolish holidays altogether, but the students rioted and managed to regain their old privileges.

All children, rich and poor, went to the same parish schools, where they were graded by ability and not birth. Teachers took immense pains to draw the very best out of their able scholars. In time these passed on to the burgh schools, where it was estimated that they spent about twice as long at their studies as did a scholar at Eton or Winchester.

A commission which examined Scottish schools in the middle of the nineteenth century found that little had changed. The inspectors admired the—

keen thoughtful faces turned towards the master, matching his every look and gesture, in the hopes of winning a place in the class, and having good news to bring home to their parents at tea time. The dux seated at the head of the class, wearing perhaps a medal; the object and envy and yet pride to all his fellows; fully conscious both of the glory and the insecurity of his position; and taught, by experience of many falls, the danger of relaxing his efforts for one moment. In front of the eager animated throng, stands the master, gaunt, muscular and time-worn, poorly clad and plain in manner and speech, but with the dignity of a ruler in his gestures and the fire of enthusiasm in his eye, never sitting down, but standing always in some commanding position before his class; full of movement, vigour and energy; so thoroughly versed in his author or his subject that he seldom requires to look at the text book, which is open in his left hand, while in his right he holds the chalk or the pointer, or perhaps flourishes the ancient tause with which in former days he used to reduce disorderly newcomers to discipline and order.

The whole system was infused with the spirit of competition. The only barriers were those of ability. The boy who wore the dux's medal might go on to become a minister or a doctor, however humble the home in which he was reared. His schooling was a ladder, on which he could climb to success. The stress on competition, however, could not but bring humiliation and unhappiness to those who gravitated in the direction of the dunce's stool.

The same Calvinist theories inspired the founding fathers

of the New England colonies, and early attempts were made to establish schools after the Scottish model. A Massachusetts law of 1647 laid down that every township of fifty or more householders should appoint a person 'to teach all such children as shall resort to him to read and write'. Further, every town of a hundred or more homes was to have a grammar school. Practice, however, did not measure up to theory. By the early nineteenth century Boston, Massachusetts, had an illiterate working class population comparable to that of a European city.

The idea of popular education was, however, gaining wide support. In 1763 the government of Prussia laid down the principle that it was the duty of the state to provide schooling for every child between the ages of five and fourteen. The American Declaration of Independence stated in round terms that government sprang from the will of the people. If the people were the fount of political authority, then it was absurd that they should be allowed to continue in ignorance. Thomas Jefferson expressed a democrat's concern with popular education.

It is an axiom in my mind that our liberties can never be safe but

Ichabod Crane's school from The Legends of Sleepy Hollow *by Washington Irving*

in the hands of the people themselves, and that, too, of the people with a certain degree of instruction.

The question at issue throughout the nineteenth century was what the 'certain degree of instruction' would be. Many argued that the common schools established for the children of workers should confine their attentions to the rudiments of reading, writing and arithmetic. It was feared that, if they stepped beyond these limits, the fabric of society would crumble. American common schools of the early nineteenth century were limited in scope and generally run on strict disciplinary lines. Pupils resented the content and methods of their schooling so bitterly that it was a frequent occurrence for them to turn and 'break up' the classrooms. Nevertheless, by the time of the Civil War, the basis had been laid for an efficient national system of education in the northern states.

The trial of strength came in the last decades of the nineteenth century. Industrial workers had exercised the right to vote for half a century; industry was making demands on higher levels of skill. Those who had been condemned to the harsh routine of the common school began to seek ways of making up for their deficiencies and to demand something better for their children. The new enthusiasm burst through the limits of official systems and spilled over into everyday life. Trades union leaders attended adult classes and workers formed themselves into discussion groups. Those who could find no official schooling did what they could to educate themselves. One writer described how he attended school with six other pupils in a tiny room in California. Their teacher's enthusiasm more than compensated for his lack of formal training.

We read Shakespeare aloud, which was all new to him and he got a tremendous kick out of it. 'By golly! That *is* good stuff!' As we went through geometry he kept about two lessons ahead. It was undiscovered territory, so he imparted his interest to us. He knew no science, but he was hungry for it, and with enthusiasm we went through Stade's *14 Weeks in Geology, in Zoology, in Chemistry*, with a box of apparatus in a little side room. He would stamp his foot in exultation and delight. It was contagious. He was the best kind of teacher because he was teaching himself and carrying us along on the wave of his enthusiasm.

Such self-help was admirable, but one major issue remained undecided. Was it the duty of a state to provide higher education for those unable to pay their own way? In 1867 the English High School at Boston began to prepare pupils for the entrance examination to the Massachusetts Institute of Technology, and within a few years other schools were following suit. This aroused strong opposition from taxpayers and the issue was taken to court. In 1872 the Kalamazoo case was heard in the Michigan Supreme Court, and judgement was given that the provision of high schools was a valid use of public money. Since the state provided universities, declared a judge, the state should also provide schools to train pupils up to the entrance standard of those universities.

The Kalamazoo judgement laid the way open for the development of the American high school as it exists today. Private schools continued, but the mass of middle class parents entrusted their children to the new schools, which offered a broadly-based and democratic educational structure. For centuries there had been opportunities available for the Scottish working class child, but he had to employ all his wits and tenacity to climb the hard *educational ladder*. The American high school offered a *broad highway* for a larger section of the population. Competition was much less fierce, so that the way could be left open for as many pupils as wished to carry on to higher studies. American teachers therefore accepted a slower pace for their classes in the interests of the average child.

The opening up of such a broad highway was naturally very expensive, and during the slump of the 1930s critics argued that it was wasteful to spread the country's resources so widely. Defenders of the system were able to point out that the high schools provided a broad band of well-qualified workers at a time when industry was becoming increasingly complex. The success of the high school experiment can be gauged from the fact that the great majority of American children now stay at school after the statutory leaving age, and no less than forty per cent go on to some form of higher education, against a mere ten per cent in Western Europe.

The democratic ideal was embedded into education

both in Scotland and the United States before the nineteenth century expansion programmes began. England, however, had a less fortunate tradition to draw upon, and any hopes that her system might develop along similar lines were dashed in the twenty years following the outbreak of the French Revolution in 1789.

The old charity schools had mostly ceased to live up to the intentions of their founders, and a poor child could only learn his letters in one of the dubious dames' schools which existed in the back streets of every town and city. The cost of instruction was but a copper or two, yet few dames' schools offered value for even such a modest sum. Teachers were, in the words of an official commission:

domestic servants out of place, discharged barmaids, vendors of toys or lollipops, keepers of small eating houses, of mangles or of small lodging houses, needlewomen who take in plain or slop work, milliners, consumptive patients in an advanced stage, cripples almost bed-ridden, persons of at least doubtful temperance, outdoor paupers, men and women of seventy or even eighty years of age, persons who spell badly (mostly women I grieve to say), who can scarcely write and who can not cipher at all.

Pupils sat on the floor and worked without any kind of equipment. Sometimes they were packed tightly enough to 'render fuel superfluous' and subdue natural high spirits in the drowsy atmosphere.

At the turn of the century a number of reformers began to organize schools for the poor which would at the same time be more efficient and based on sound religious principles. But England was at war with revolutionary France and the smallest change in the fabric of society was branded as dangerous Jacobinism. Critics argued that an educated worker would soon get above his place. He would refuse to serve the rich as custom decreed, and before long would espouse the cause of revolution.

The reformers defended themselves against such imputations. Their sole aim, they declared, was to teach the workers true virtue, among which respect for their betters would feature prominently. They based their instruction on the time-honoured 'Divine Law of Subordination', which was to be given classic expression in a verse of Mrs Alexander's well-known hymn.

The rich man in his castle,
The poor man at his gate.
God made them high and lowly
And gave them their estate.
　　All things bright and beautiful, etc.

A nineteenth century Lancastrian monitorial system: (a) groups of children read to monitors from charts; (b) monitors lead pupils to seats—note hats hanging on backs to save time and cloakrooms; (c) monitors inspects written work at signal 'Show slates'

Armed with such impeccable aims, the movement for popular education grew in strength during the early decades of the nineteenth century. Two religious societies, representing Anglican and Nonconformist interests, were formed to spread the benefits of education among the poor. They were, however, faced with an immense task, as industrial communities like Leeds and Manchester were spreading at an enormous rate. As has been seen, the churches were not prepared to hand over to the state the advantages which they had won, yet they did not have the financial resources to match their task.

The main cost of education lay in teachers' salaries, so the *monitorial system* was introduced to cut down this expense. Two men, Joseph Lancaster and Andrew Bell, laid claim to the dubious honour of having invented the method. The former claimed with pride that, by using his system, one teacher would be able to look after up to 1,000 children at a time. The factory system had invaded the schoolroom. The teacher concentrated on drilling a number of older children, or monitors, to learn a lesson off by heart. They in their turn drilled the younger pupils, while the teacher hovered in the background, ready to mete out punishment to any child who stepped out of line. The system had to be highly regimented. Pupils sat down, stood up, lifted their books and put them down again, all on a word of command. Those who learnt well were given badges or offices within the school; those who stumbled over their recitation had to stand in the corner, wearing the dunce's cap; some were even shackled for their sins.

The Second Reform Bill of 1867 extended the right to vote to members of the industrial working class, and it was recognized that the state could not abdicate responsibility for popular education any longer. The Whig politician Robert Lowe announced with polished sarcasm, 'We must educate our masters'. The religious societies had failed to meet the needs of the growing population, and in 1870—just 107 years after Prussia—the English Parliament brought a system of state education into being. The Education Act of that year laid down that schools should be set up in areas where they were not provided by the religious societies, and that these new schools were to be under the care of elected

A nineteenth century Ragged School

school boards.

At last it became possible for every child to have a rudimentary education, but the new system offered neither a broad highway, nor an educational ladder to higher things. No matter how able he might be, the working class child had no prospect of passing beyond the elementary schooling provided for him. Grammar schools were all fee-paying, and a labourer's wages left nothing to spare for education.

As in America, pressure began to build up from below. Workers argued that education was their children's birth-right, not a privilege bestowed upon them by their social betters.

Before the end of the century a number of progressive school boards were experimenting along the American lines.

Rather than try to break open the grammar schools, it seemed preferable to open higher grade schools, paid for out of the school rate, which would take children across the gulf between elementary schools and the seats of higher learning. Higher grade schools were founded in several cities—but once again the legality of such expenditure was challenged in the courts. Mr Justice Wills delivered a judgement exactly opposite to that of the Michigan court. The idea, he declared, that school boards were—

free to teach at the expense of the ratepayers to adults and children indiscriminately the higher mathematics, advanced chemistry, both theoretical and practical, political economy, art of a kind wholly beyond anything that can be taught to children, French, German, History and I know not what, appears to me to be the *ne plus ultra* of extravagance.

Pressure from public opinion and within the teaching profession became so great that it was soon clear that the rigid class segregation of English education could not continue. The government would not, however, consider setting up a broad highway on the American pattern. The solution, brought in by Act of Parliament in 1902, was to allow a small number of able children to go on scholarship from elementary to grammar schools.

This was an important break-through and many working class children took the opportunity offered. A fair number, however, found the ladder hard to climb and fell by the wayside. After passing the competitive examination, they were absorbed into a middle class school, where behaviour patterns were different from those to which they were accustomed. With loyalties divided, children were sometimes faced with the need to reject either home or school.

R. A. Butler and his colleagues in the war-time coalition government made a serious attempt to overcome the inequalities so long built into English education, when they introduced the Education Act of 1944. They established the principle that free secondary education should be made available for all, and the school to which any child went would be determined by his ability and not by his parents' capacity to pay. Gifted children would go to grammar schools; those with more limited ability to technical or secondary modern schools. Institutions were to be different by nature of the special needs of their pupils, but each would be held in 'parity of esteem' with the others.

Unfortunately the class divisions of centuries could not be so destroyed by a legislative stroke. It certainly became easier for a working class child to go on to higher education, but the English educational system remained substantially like a three-tier wedding cake. The secondary modern schools, retaining many of the characteristics of the old elementary schools, drew overwhelmingly from the working class. The grammar schools remained true to their middle class traditions. At the top, for those who could afford to opt out of the state system altogether, the public schools continued to provide a royal road to social status and well-paid jobs.

The Labour Party, which had fully supported the 1944 Act, began to consider methods of bringing the different sections of society closer together. In some areas bilateral schools were set up, which contained grammar and secondary departments on a single campus. It was at last decided that even this was inadequate, and in 1964 the party came into power on an election promise to take the country over to a comprehensive system.

The following years have seen a major overhaul of secondary education, which is still far from complete. The ideal of the broad highway has been widely accepted by both the teaching profession and the public. The practical problems of implementing the change remain, however, very great. The most formidable is the problem of size. A grammar or a secondary modern school could function efficiently with 500 pupils or less. The size of a comprehensive school, however, is governed by the efficiency of its sixth form unit. If it draws pupils from a true cross-section of the population, it needs about 1,000 pupils before the sixth form becomes large enough to offer an adequate range of courses.

Various solutions have been tried to meet this problem. Some comprehensives are forced to do the best they can with their pupils spread over several sets of buildings; others have been divided into separate 'middle' and 'upper' schools. The economical solution is to create a sixth form college drawing from a number of smaller schools. Head teachers, however, have generally been reluctant to see their schools decapitated, and qualified staff resist any suggestion that they should sacrifice their sixth form teaching.

There are few who would quarrel with the American John Dewey's definition of aim.

What the best and wisest parent wants for his own child, that must the community want for all its children.

The issue at stake is how far governments are prepared to back up such ideals. If more education is offered to children, more will be accepted, and the tax payer has to meet the bill. British governments in particular have a depressing record of trying to solve economic crises by wielding the axe in educational expenditure. If the pattern continues, no amount of remodelling of schools will establish a broad highway of educational opportunity.

Opponents of present policy echo the phrase coined by novelist Kingsley Amis, 'more means worse'. They argue that broadening of opportunity can only be achieved by reducing standards at the top. Such evidence as there is, however, suggests that the educational system is still far from exploiting reserves of talent to the full, and that outstanding pupils can be drawn from sections of society which have so far been effectively cut off from higher education.

Perhaps a more serious cause for concern is the provision in a comprehensive system for the small number of pupils endowed with rare qualities of intellectual or artistic genius. The Russians, for all their espousal of rigid egalitarian principles, are experimenting with special schools in which intensive training is given to top mathematicians and scientists of the future. In England, however, the issue is confused by the long tradition of élitist education, and suggestions of selection of any sort are summarily dismissed by protagonists of the comprehensive system. It is now recognized that children of exceptional ability, like those at the other end of the scale, need special provision. Whether this should be given within the comprehensive school or in intensive units outside it must remain a question for experiment and debate.

7. Teaching the Daughter

A girl should be taught to sew and not to read, unless one wishes to make a nun of her.

OLD ITALIAN PROVERB

'IT doesn't matter so much for a girl, does it?' Those words, which express the attitude of the whole of western civilization towards the education of women, are still spoken by many parents. It doesn't matter—girls have a role as wives and mothers to which the formal education of the classroom can at best make a fringe contribution. Such has been the assumption of the majority of parents throughout history.

While man's primitive function was to hunt and defend the home, woman bore his children and prepared his food. In some societies she also tilled the fields and acted as a beast of burden. It has been remarked that the traditional picture of Joseph fleeing into Egypt with Mary on a donkey by his side is wrong. In first century Palestine Joseph would have been on the donkey! Even when the men qualified for training as members of the élite, their wives had little more education than if they were married to a peasant. While the Jews honoured the mother of the family, the father was both priest and teacher, and no woman would have considered encroaching on his domain.

Plato was the first to take women's education seriously. In his republic women were to carry babies only because nature offered no alternative. The ties of mother love were quickly cut after birth. In compensation women were allowed to take their place alongside men in all aspects of the guardian's training. If need arose they even had to be prepared to carry arms against the enemies of the state. Plato saw no reason why women should not rise to positions of authority if they proved themselves worthy. But Aristotle expressed the more general view when he repudiated his master's teaching and declared that man must rule and woman obey.

Roman literature certainly does not give the impression that all women were ignorant and down-trodden. It can be assumed that many high-born girls learnt to read and write with their brothers, though they did not go on to study rhetoric because they had no call to give formal speeches. Their education was given in the home with their mothers and the women slaves, where they learnt the arts which would be useful to them in later life. There are records of women professors teaching in the Athenian Academy, but the last of the line was lynched by a Christian mob in A.D. 415.

A comparison between ancient times and the Middle Ages hardly justifies the common claim that Christianity improved the position of woman in society. The chastity belt and the scold's bridle were obscene symbols of her subjection to man. The records provide an occasional glimpse of an educated woman, like Abelard's Heloise, but the general picture is very bleak.

Even within the cloistered life women do not seem to have attained any great level of education. The nunneries appear to have had no libraries—no manuscripts have come to light written by a woman's hand, no chronicles tell the story of the times from a female point of view. When a bishop visited a monastery he delivered his charge in Latin; in a nunnery he had to speak simply in the vernacular. It may, therefore, be doubted whether the girls from noble families who went to a nunnery to be 'finished' received any education there worthy of the name.

According to the code of chivalry the woman was essentially a decorative object. Her function, as Rousseau said later, was to be pleasing in man's sight, 'to win his respect and love, to train him in childhood, to tend him in manhood, to counsel and console, to make his life pleasant and happy'.

At the Renaissance some men began to question this negative role. Thomas More, Lord Chancellor of England and friend of Erasmus, decided to use marriage as a testing ground for his modern theories. He chose himself a bride of seventeen, who had been brought up in the country in order that—

he might more easily mould her to his own tastes. He began to interest her in books and music, to accustom her to repeat the substance of sermons she heard, and to train her to other useful accomplishments. All this was quite new to the girl. She had been brought up at home in complete idleness, playing and talking to the servants. Very soon she began to be bored, and refused to comply. If her husband urged her, she would burst into tears; sometimes even throwing herself to the ground and beating her head on the floor, as though she wished to die. As this went on, the young man, concealing his vexation suggested that they should pay a visit to her parents in the country, with which she joyfully fell in. On arrival he left her with her mother and sisters, and went off with her father to hunt. As soon as the two were alone, he told his story: how instead of the happy companion he had hoped for, he found his wife perpetually in tears and quite intractable; and he begged for assistance in curing her.

'I have given her to you,' was the reply, 'and she is yours. If she doesn't obey you, use your rights and beat her into a better frame of mind.'

'I know,' said the husband, 'what my rights are; but I would rather the change were effected with your aid and authority, than resort to such extreme measures.'

The father consented, and after a day or two found an opportunity to speak with his daughter alone. Setting his face to severity he said:

'You are a plain child, with no particular charm; and I used often to be afraid I should have difficulty in getting you a husband. After a great deal of trouble I found you one whom any woman might envy; a man who, if he weren't very kind, would hardly consider you worth having as a servant; and then you rebel against him.'

And with this he grew so angry that he seemed about to beat her: all of course, in pretense, for he is a clever actor. The girl was frightened, and also moved by the truth of what he had said. Falling at his feet, she vowed to do better in future; and he promised continuance of his affection, if she would keep her word. Then returning to her husband, whom she found alone in his room, she fell down before him and said:

'Until now I have known neither you nor myself. Henceforward you shall find me quite different: only forget what is past.'

He sealed her repentance with a kiss; and in this happy state of mind she continued till her death.

Undeterred by initial difficulties, More persevered, and his daughter Margaret was said to have been the most cultured woman of her age. Henry VIII was influenced by these new ideas and determined to see that his daughters had the best teaching available. The Spanish writer, Vives, was enlisted as tutor for the elder daughter, Mary. Vives, who realized that he could be teaching a future queen of England, took his responsibilities very seriously and wrote the first book on the teaching of women. It was only because women were given no education, he declared, that they were for the most part—

hard to please, studious and most diligent to adorn themselves, marvellers of trifles, in prosperity proud and insolent, in adversity abject and feeble; and for lack of good learning, they love and hate that only the which they learned of their unlearned mothers.

Vives' own pupil was not an outstanding example of this new interest in women's education. Her half-sister Elizabeth, however, was a woman of culture, able to hold her own in any company. Shakespeare drew a picture of this new pattern of Renaissence womanhood in Beatrice, heroine of *Much Ado About Nothing*. Sharp-witted and cultured—like Elizabeth I, she finds the course of true love a thorny one.

The 'Carved Parlour' of Campden House School, Kensington

From the sixteenth century onwards, the noble girl could receive a sound education from a private tutor in her own home. In practice, however, the hard business of book learning was generally neglected on the grounds that it 'did not matter for a girl'. A few charity schools were supposed to offer opportunities of a sort, but as time passed they generally degenerated into sweat shops where illiterate girls worked through the hours of daylight doing needlework which was sold to provide the wages for semi-literate teachers. A number of private schools existed for the daughters of the 'middling' classes of society. Of these a few offered sound education but most concerned themselves only with details of deportment and good manners; they taught 'a little music, a little singing, a little French, a little ornamental work and nothing else'.

It was seriously argued that a woman's brain was inadequate to cope with mathematics, beyond the first four rules of arithmetic. If a girl possessed an understanding of politics or business she had to disguise the fact for fear of being charged with unladylike presumption. If she possessed a strong and athletic body, she had to encase it in corsets, and learn to adopt the statuesque poses laid down in the rules of decorum.

The campaign for women's rights is generally associated with the names of Emmeline and Christabel Pankhurst, and with the decade before 1914. The true pioneers of the movement, however, were not sufragettes but teachers, who laid the foundation for equality a full half century earlier.

As would be expected, the United States set the pace in the new movement. In 1838 the authorities at Oberlin College took the remarkable step of opening its advanced classes to women as well as men, and before long other schools and colleges were under pressure to follow suit. Long-established institutions in New England resisted the pressure and women had to set up their own schools and colleges. In the expanding Middle West, where it was unthinkable that every school should be duplicated, co-education was rapidly accepted as the natural educational pattern, and before long this established itself as the norm of American education.

The struggle was more bitterly fought in England, but by

F

the middle of the century a handful of influential men had been won over to the idea of women's education. The argument was first presented on a very limited front: many parents employed governesses who were responsible for the early stages of education of both boys and girls. It was, however, obvious that these governesses were woefully ill prepared for the task. Supporters of women's education argued that employers could reasonably expect to see a certificate of proficiency from applicants.

Queen Victoria, a redoubtable foe of women's rights, was prevailed upon to lend her name to a new college which opened in London in 1848.

We have been graciously pleased to permit the name of Queen's College, in which certificates of qualification are granted to governesses, and in which arrangements have been made with professors of high talent in society to open classes in all branches of female education.

One of the first pupils was an artist's daughter called Frances Mary Buss. Still only nineteen, she had no less than five years teaching experience behind her, and she continued teaching throughout her two-year course. In the evenings, after a day's work in school, she would set off from the middle class suburb of Camden Town and trudge across London to Queen's College, where she attended lectures by well known scholars like F. D. Maurice, its first principal.

In 1850, armed with her certificate of proficiency, she announced that she was opening a new school for girls in North London. She aimed to attract the daughters of the middle classes, and based her venture on the belief that

a sound education, based on religious principles, is as necessary for the daughters as for the sons of the large and influential portion of society consisting of Professional Gentlemen of limited means, clerks in public and private offices and persons engaged in Trade and other pursuits.

Miss Buss herself was no enemy of the idea of mixed schooling, and she recorded the 'real heartache' which she felt when she dismissed all thought of marriage from her mind. But she had to recognize facts. In the climate of her times mixed education was dubbed immoral, and she would have been unable to fulfil her ambitions as a married woman.

'The Giant Stride in the Gymnasium', North London Collegiate School, 1882

Parents soon realized that she offered girls a higher level of schooling than they could get elsewhere. 'I am sure girls can learn anything they are taught in an interesting manner and for which they have a motive to work,' declared Miss Buss, and she arranged her curriculum accordingly. When asked whether girls and boys should learn the same things, she would simply reply that she had no idea what boys were capable of achieving. For her girls only the best would do.

Alongside the new educational opportunities was a new physical emancipation, symbolized by the Giant Stride in the gymnasium. Twice a week, at 8.30 in the morning, a certain Captain Chiasso came to put the girls through their paces. Frances Buss's emphasis on physical training may have led some of her disciples to adopt a somewhat over 'hearty' approach, but in 1850 it was an essential reaction against the old enslavement to ladylike decorum.

A past pupil described the excitement of the early days, when pupils and teachers felt themselves pioneers in a new experiment. The girls came from 'respectable' homes, but many had to walk long distances to and from school.

Do we not remember the overskirts insisted on by Miss Buss as a protection from the wet, at a time when waterproof clothing was unknown? What dressing and undressing went on round the stove, where Miss Reneau sat with the default list, to put down the name of any too riotous girl! What a delight the giant strides and see-saws were to the athletic young damsels of the period.

North London set the tone for a luxuriant growth of middle class schools in all parts of the country. There was also a demand for a more 'select' kind of education, after the pattern of the boys' public schools. In 1858 Frances Buss's contemporary at Queen's College, Dorothea Beale, was appointed head of Cheltenham Ladies' College, where she had a long and influential career, extending the privileges of emancipation to the daughters of the well-to-do.

Identified as they were with the growing campaign for women's suffrage, these educational pioneers aroused deep resentment in male circles. W. S. Gilbert devoted the whole of his opera *Princess Ida* to heaping scorn on women's education. His heroes express the male attitude in the new sex war.

FLORIAN.

A woman's college! Maddest folly going!
What can girls learn within its walls worth knowing?
I'll lay a crown (the Princess shall decide it)
I'll teach them twice as much in half an hour outside it.

HILARION.

Hush scoffer, ere you sound your puny thunder
List to their aims, and bow your heads in wonder . . .

As for fashion they forswear it
    So they say—so they say—
And the circle—they will square it
    Some fine day—some fine day—
Then the little pigs they're teaching
    For to fly—for to fly—
And the niggers they'll be bleaching
    By and bye—by and bye.
Each newly joined aspirant
    To the clan—to the clan—
Must repudiate the tyrant
    Known as man—known as man—
They mock at him and flout him,
For they do not care about him,
And they're going to do without him,
    If they can—if they can!

Although these unattractive words never achieved the popularity of some of Gilbert's other work, they spoke for a large body of conservative opinion.

The blue-stocking image has stayed with women's education into the twentieth century. Co-education was slow to catch on in Britain, and save for the shadowy figure of the school chaplain, girls' schools remained all-female institutions. In the early days pupils chanted:

> Miss Buss and Miss Beale
> Cupid's darts do not feel.
> How diffcrent from us
> Miss Beale and Miss Buss.

An anti-sex aura was bound to cling around girls' schools as long as the staff consisted wholly of spinsters. Until the Second World War a woman had to give up teaching as soon as she married, but the influx of married women into the profession since 1939 has helped greatly to reassure girls that their schools are in touch with real life.

It would, however, be wrong to suggest that anything like equality has been achieved. In Britain far more girls than boys leave school as soon as it is possible for them to do so, and only half as many girls go on to university courses as boys. The situation in the applied sciences is particularly bleak. In Soviet Russia 20% of all qualified engineers are women; in France the proportion is 2%; in Britain it is .2%.

One of the more interesting discussions within the teaching profession today is how far girls and boys really do need different teaching methods and a different content to the syllabus. They mature at unequal rates, and have distinctive 'male' and 'female' attitudes to life. The female sex has still produced no painter or composer of universally acknowledged genius, though as writers and interpretive artists they compete with men on equal terms. Much of the difference undoubtedly exists because children play out the roles which society imposes on them. In Russia, where it is accepted that women should fight and men should dance, the gap in achievement between the sexes has narrowed remarkably. The traditions of chivalry die hard, but members of the younger generation are becoming impatient of the old male-dominated society.

Women have been held back in the past because of their specialized child-bearing functions, but it is precisely because girls will become mothers that their education is of special importance. If you teach a girl, you have taken a fair step towards teaching a whole family of the next generation. As modern labour-saving devices lighten the load of drudgery in the home, women have greatly increased opportunities to extend the scope of their lives; they need the fullest preparation for work and leisure that education can provide.

8. Teaching the Child

Experienced parents, when children's rights are preached to them, very naturally ask whether children are to be allowed to do what they like. The best reply is to ask whether adults are to be allowed to do what they like. The two cases are the same.

GEORGE BERNARD SHAW

TODAY we live in a world in which children *as children* have a right to exist. When they are babies they live in nurseries, decorated with pictures in bold shapes and bright colours; when they can read they are given books specially written and illustrated to suit their interests and achievements. Every big store has a department given over to serviceable and gaily-coloured clothes designed for the young.

We take these things for granted, and indeed sometimes children's tastes are exploited for commercial ends. Two hundred years ago, however, this was unheard of. Little limbs were stiffly encased in shrunken versions of adult fashions; small waists were pinched by corsets and youngsters' wigs were laid out to be powdered alongside their fathers. Children lived on sufferance in an adults' world, and were constantly made to realize the fact.

Both the classical and the Christian traditions of education had contributed to this state of affairs. The Greeks and Romans looked on childhood as a regrettable state, to be got through as quickly as possible. Classical writers showed no interest in children or their emotions. Education was simply a process of training adults, and it was taken for granted that the process would be a painful one.

The church added its dismal contribution with the doctrine of original sin. Since man was born evil, it was clearly wrong to pander to the whims of childhood. The natural emotions of man had to be overlaid as quickly and efficiently as possible by instruction and discipline.

77

The repudiation of this point of view came as part of a much bigger movement of which the French Revolution was the most obvious product. Its watchword was freedom, and its high priest was the French philosopher Rousseau. He proclaimed that childhood was the most formative and exciting period of life, and children should not be stifled or suppressed by adults.

> Love childhood, indulge its sports, its pleasures, its delightful instincts . . . Why rob these innocents of the joys which pass so quickly, of that precious gift which they cannot abuse? . . . As soon as they are aware of the joys of life let them rejoice in it.
>
> Let them run, jump and shout to their heart's content. All their activities are instincts of the body for its growth and strength.

He turned the doctrine of original sin on its head and declared that children were born innocent, and became contaminated by contact with the adult world. William Wordsworth, expressed the new dogma in poetry.

> Heaven lies about us in our infancy!
> Shades of the prison house begin to close
>   Upon the growing boy,
> But he beholds the light, and whence it flows,
>   He sees it in his joy;
> The youth, who daily further from the east
> Must travel, still is nature's priest,
>   And by the vision splendid
>   Is on his way attended;
> At length the man perceives it die away,
> And fade into the light of common day.

Rousseau was a failure as a teacher, but he expressed his views on education in his *Emile*, which must take its place alongside Plato's *Republic* as one of the cornerstones of educational thought. It takes the form of a detailed account of the education of the young Emile, but Rousseau never expected his readers to take it too literally. It was the declaration of a new attitude which started from the principle 'begin thus by making a more careful study of your scholars, for it is clear that you know nothing about them'. As a rough guide he advised teachers to find out what the current educational practice was—and do exactly the opposite.

The first twelve years of a child's life were to be spent in the open country air and free from formal instruction.

Give nature time to work before you take over her business, lest you interfere with her dealings. You assert that you know the value of time and are afraid to waste it. You fail to perceive that it is a greater waste of time to use it ill than to do nothing, and that a child ill-taught is further from virtue than a child who has learned nothing at all. You are afraid to see him spend his early years doing nothing. What! is it nothing to be happy, nothing to run and jump all day?

In practice, however, the child would be learning as he watched the sun rise and helped the gardener with his work. He would be encouraged to find out the answers to his questions for himself. Thus at twelve 'his ideas are few but precise. He knows nothing by rote but much by experience'.

Not all the ideas in *Emile* were new, but at the end of the eighteenth century the world was ready for them. Conservative opinion was profoundly shocked and a copy of the book was publicly burnt by order of the Archbishop of Paris. But the ideas in it caught the imagination of liberal-minded men and women. Among these was a Swiss called Pestalozzi. He found that Rousseau put the realities of contemporary education into stark focus.

My own visionary tendencies were stimulated to a pitch of extraordinary enthusiasm when I read that dream book of his. I compared the education which I had received at home and at school with that which Rousseau demanded for Emile and felt how wretchedly inadequate it all was.

Rousseau preached that man should return to nature and Pestalozzi determined to follow his advice. He bought a house in the country, and opened it to twenty poor children. He intended 'to live for years like a beggar among beggars, in order to teach them to live like men'. His intention was fulfilled all too literally. He had no head for business, and even in the country there were men ready to cheat him out of his slender funds. Before long he had reduced himself and his family to absolute poverty, and they survived with difficulty, living off what they could grow in their garden.

Pestalozzi was fifty-three years old before he had another chance of putting the new ideas into practice. In 1798 the French revolutionary army pillaged a Swiss town leaving many children homeless and destitute. The authorities asked Citizen Pestalozzi to care for them. The children arrived at the deserted convent assigned to them in the autumn of that year.

Many came with scabies of long standing so that they could hardly walk, many with open sores on their heads, many in rags crawling with vermin, many so thin that one could count all their bones, sallow, stupefied, with fear in their eyes and wrinkles of distrust and anxiety on their brows; some were bold and arrogant, habitual beggars, liars and cheats; others were crushed by their misery, meek but suspicious, frightened and glum.

Pestalozzi had eighty children on his hands for whom he had to be teacher, sick nurse, parent—everything. 'They were with me, and I was with them. I had nothing, no house, no friends, no servants, I only had them.' Yet before the spring sun began to melt the snow on the Swiss mountains, Pestalozzi had transformed his community through his own immense capacity for giving love. The children were no longer frightened, and had learned how to be considerate of one another, while their teacher, till then the prey of bouts of depression, was blissfully happy living among them.

This first school was closed for political reasons, but Pestalozzi had proved that freedom could work. In his last years he was head of schools at Bergdorf and Yverdon. Before long he had become famous, and people arrived from all over Europe and as far away as America to see him at work. He was not a clear thinker or a good writer, but visitors went away with two ideas impressed on their minds. In the first place, all teaching had to grow out of a deep love for children. Secondly, instruction should work through the child's awareness of concrete objects—he should be allowed to touch things and see things for himself and not just be fed on an endless diet of words.

Among Pestalozzi's visitors was the Scotsman Andrew Bell, joint inventor of the monitorial system. At the end of his tour he turned to the interpreter and announced, 'Now I understand the method of your Pestalozzi. Believe me, sir, in twelve years it will not be mentioned, while mine will be spread over the whole world.' Of all countries, Britain was most resistant to Pestalozzi's ideas, but incredibly, in 1880 an English lecturer was able to state, 'We have learned what he had to teach, and we are far beyond him.' Certainly the ideas of the 'object lesson' had penetrated even to the remote world of Mr Wackford Squeers—but their application would hardly have satisfied the reformers.

'This is the first class in English spelling and philosophy, Nickleby,' said Squeers, beckoning Nicholas to stand beside him 'We'll get up a Latin one and hand that over to you. Now, then, where's the first boy?'

'Please, sir, he's cleaning the back-parlour window,' said the temporary head of the philosophical class.

'So he is, to be sure,' rejoined Squeers. 'We go upon the practical mode of teaching, Nickleby; the regular education system. C-l-e-a-n, clean, verb active, to make bright, to scour. W-i-n, win, d-e-r, der, winder, a casement. When the boy knows this out of a book, he goes and does it.'

It is to be feared that in other establishments besides Dotheboys Hall many hours of profitless labour have been justified on the grounds of practical education, but those who adopted the true spirit of Pestalozzi found children responding to education with new interest.

The next step was taken by Froebel, who started his teaching career as a member of Pestalozzi's staff. When he branched out on his own he developed a particular interest in teaching the youngest age group.

All the child is ever to be and become, (he wrote) lies, however slightly indicated, in the child, and can be attained only through development from within outward.

For centuries children's play had been at best, tolerated, and at worst, forbidden altogether. Obeying Rousseau's instruction to study the child, Froebel decided that play was the highest form of activity possible at that stage of development. It was a deeply serious occupation in which lay the seeds of all future development.

A child that plays, thoroughly, with self-active determination, perseveringly until fatigue forbids, will surely be a thorough, determined man, capable of self sacrifice for the promotion of the welfare of himself and others. Is not the most beautiful expression of child life at this time a playing child?—a child wholly absorbed in his play?—a child that has fallen asleep while so absorbed?

Froebel constructed the first 'system' of teaching. Some admirers tended to follow it too closely, assuming that, after the master had spoken, no further development could take place. But through his influence freedom of expression began to work into schools from the lowest age group upwards.

The new approach to childhood brought hope to many who had previously been condemned as society's outcasts. Dedicated men and women began to work on principles for teaching handicapped children, who in earlier generations

Contemporary infants' school children at play

Infants' school children enacting a play, 1905; Froebel's principles were already coming into use

would have begged in the streets or lain huddled in the corner of some institution. Pestalozzi had shown that all the senses could be used in teaching, so the fact that the sight or the hearing was blocked meant that the other senses should be developed to a new pitch of awareness. In France, Séguin even showed that unexpected results could be gained from teaching the mentally defective.

Towards the end of the nineteenth century a young woman doctor was walking down a street in Rome when she came upon a beggar woman with a child. The woman pushed out her hands and asked for money, but the child was completely abstracted, playing with tiny scraps of coloured paper. Maria Montessori never lost the picture of that child. She took up work teaching mentally defective children on Séguin's principles, and at the end of two years was able to present her pupils for a public examination alongside normal children. Everyone was impressed by her achievement but Montessori looked at it from the opposite point of view.

Whilst everyone was admiring my idiots I was searching for reasons which could keep back the healthy and happy children of the ordinary schools on so low a plane that they could be equalled in tests of intelligence by my unfortunate pupils.

From this the idea came to her that the methods developed

for use with defective children might be of assistance in teaching those with normal mental equipment.

The opportunity to try out her ideas arrived when a building society erected a new block of flats in the slums of Rome. It was decided that it would be cheaper to provide a nursery for the children of the tenants, than to repair the damage they would do if allowed to run wild. Maria Montessori was given charge of the school and allowed to develop it on her own lines. She had no money to buy desks, so she had low wooden tables and chairs made; she also provided each child with a little arm chair. The pupils arrived for the opening in their blue orphan smocks:

sixty tearful, frightened children, so shy that it was impossible to get them to speak; their faces were expressionless, with bewildered eyes, as though they had never seen anything in their lives.

In the classroom were the objects which had been used so

Maria Montessori watches two children playing at work with her Method

successfully with defective children. Montessori immediately noticed that there was a difference between the two groups of children. With the defectives the teacher had to use the objects as an *aid* to instruction; but the normal children did not need the teacher's help—they went up to them, handled them and became utterly absorbed in their work. Like Froebel, she was struck by the way that such activity could draw them into a state of utter contentment.

The two key factors of the Montessori Method had already emerged. The classroom was a 'house of childhood'—all its furniture was to be on the child's scale, all its fittings and equipment within easy reach. It would be gaily decked with flowers so that the child would feel that it was a natural and happy environment in which to work. The second feature was that the teacher would withdraw from the limelight and leave the children in direct contact with the objects from which they were to learn. Discipline became a state of happy activity rather than a condition of order imposed from above.

From the Children's Homes the old-time teacher who wore herself out maintaining discipline of immobility and wasting her breath in loud and continual discourse, has disappeared, and the didactic material which contains within itself the control of errors is substituted, making auto-education possible to each child.

The illiterate parents in Montessori's slum tenement were amazed when the King and Queen of Italy came to see their children at work. Educationalists, too, arrived from many parts of the world. From the time of Pestalozzi Americans had taken a particular interest in the new methods, and the principles worked out in the experimental schools had been widely put into practice in their schools. Many of the ideas were further developed by a research team in Chicago headed by John Dewey. He was anxious to ensure that the liberty introduced into schools was based on a firm foundation. It was useless for a teacher to talk of freedom if he did not then provide the children with objects which would make that freedom productive.

He worked out the project system, based on a single centre of interest. The project might start from an activity which the pupils could enjoy and understand, like cooking. From this practical activity they could be led to examine the simple chemical events which took place in the process—to study the plants which went into the ingredients—to find out where those plants were grown—to carry out research into the historical inventions which had made the process possible—to measure and calculate the ingredients which were used. In this way the old subjects of the curriculum became unified in a single search for knowledge. He insisted that everything must have a purpose, and warned against the casual projects—which still all too often shelter under his authority—in which any advance of the child's powers is purely accidental.

Children worked in an atmosphere more like a workshop than the conventional classroom. They were encouraged to help each other, so that the stigma of 'cheating' became a thing of the past. Under the old system, he argued:

the place where children are sent for discipline is the one place in the world where it is most difficult to get experience—the mother of all discipline worth the name.

Like Montessori, he found that order sprang naturally out of activity and mutual respect.

At Summerhill School in Suffolk, A. S. Neill has taken the concept of freedom to its logical conclusion. His school is run by a council of pupils and staff, in which his own vote counts for no more than that of the youngest child. He has renounced compulsion, and holds to his principles rigidly. No child is forced to attend lessons, but most choose to do so of their own free will; the only school rules are those which have been freely accepted by the council for the good of the whole community. From this experience of responsibility Neill expects children to learn to live together happily, to respect other people's property and feelings.

Once a woman brought her girl of seven to see me. 'Mr Neill,' she said, 'I have read every line you have written; and even before Daphne was born, I had decided to bring her up exactly along your lines.'

I glanced at Daphne who was standing on my grand piano with her heavy shoes on. She made a leap for the sofa and nearly went through the springs. 'You see how natural she is,' said the mother. 'The Neillian child!' I fear that I blushed.

Freedom and licence can look alike, but in reality they are mutually exclusive. A. S. Neill seeks to bring children to maturity by thrusting all the responsibility back on them. His methods are highly controversial, and critics argue that it is unfair to train children to expect a freedom they will not experience in adult life. A sixteen-year-old girl in another progressive school complained that, while pupils were theoretically being trained for the big wide world, in practice 'we're very feather-bedded and our rat-race is only 100 yards, with no hurdles'. Neill would reply that the fact that adult life is a rat-race is no justification for bringing tension into childhood as well. Children, he declares, will find their own level, if left to themselves.

Many experienced teachers would wish to challenge this assertion and Neill himself admits that it does not work out so well with children of limited ability. It has been demonstrated that children of average ability or below who have not learned to read and write by the age of ten, are likely to have difficulty with these basic skills for the rest of their lives. Compulsion is a loaded word which brings back memories of floggings and the dunce's cap. To Neill the modern teacher's 'Wouldn't it be nice if we . . .' expresses compulsion as much as the old-fashioned 'you must'. Yet most teachers will find themselves in situations where pressure of some sort has to be used. Few children are free to opt out of lessons altogether, but the kind of openness and comradeship which Neill has achieved at Summerhill is a model to the profession, as the schools of Pestalozzi, Froebel and Montessori have provided models in the past.

It is a by-product of the open approach to education that pupils should come to expect a greater share in shaping their own education. It would be a pity if grosser manifestations of 'student power' should cause public opinion to react against this natural development. At the same time the teacher has a right to point out that the end product of education is an adult and not a child. He fails in his task if he becomes so entranced with childhood or identified with youth that he sacrifices his position as an adult in the classroom community. When this happens the children for whom he has responsibility lose the security on which their growth depends.

Rousseau's instruction to 'study children' has been taken increasingly seriously in the past century. The writings of

G

Sigmund Freud gave a new significance to childhood, for it became recognized that impressions gained in the early years of development could be immensely important in later life. Since Freud's time, countless detailed studies have been made of children suffering from behaviour problems. It has been amply demonstrated that children act out the stresses in their lives by aggressive or anti-social behaviour and that the punishments traditionally handed out in remedy can be positively harmful. Many teachers are still mistrustful of these findings, and even those who accept them in principle often find it hard to reconcile the needs of an individual child with the welfare of the larger group.

Child study has also been directed onto the achievements and abilities of the normal child. In the 1930s psychologists were confident that they were able to isolate a fixed 'intelligence quotient' in any individual by a means of specially prepared tests. The 1944 English Education Act was drawn up under the influence of this theory and terms like 'the eleven plus' and 'I.Q.' became standard jargon of a generation of educationalists. Recent experiments, however, have proved that tests work on a broad margin of error and have even cast doubt on the very concept of fixed intelligence. Other less-publicised child study projects will probably have greater long-term influence on teaching. Perhaps most notable has been the work of Piaget, who plotted the ages at which children are able to absorb different levels of knowledge. From his work has come the alarming conclusion that many teachers try to put across concepts which their pupils are *incapable* of understanding.

The 'new methods'—which are now nearly 200 years old—have by no means routed the old. They have brought rapid advances in infant and junior teaching, and they are making their appearance in secondary schools—mainly among the younger age group and in forms for less able children. In Britain the most notable development in the 1960s has been the introduction of the Nuffield Maths and Science project which works on principles developed from Dewey. It is not necessarily reactionary to argue that older children still benefit from a certain amount of formal teaching. One thing is certain—no student entering training college today can expect to be provided with methods of teaching which will last him unchanged throughout his career.

9. Teaching the Teacher

Who shall teach the schoolmaster? Who shall impress a pedagogue with a due sense of his deficiencies?

THOMAS HAMILTON, 1833

UNTIL the beginning of the nineteenth century there were few who argued that training was a necessary part of a teacher's equipment. A visitor to an Alsace village some two hundred years ago sought out the school-master and asked him what he taught the children. 'Nothing, sir,' came the reply. 'Why, then, were you made a school-master?' he asked. 'Why, sir, I had been taking care of the pigs for the countryside for many years, and when I got too old and feeble for that, they sent me here to take care of the children.'

A few prophetic individuals had seen that some sort of training was essential. Richard Mulcaster, High Master of St Paul's at the end of the sixteenth century, for instance, recommended that all teachers should go to the university, and then proceed to a special college for vocational training. But no one took his advice seriously and those who wished to influence other members of the teaching profession could only write books and hope that these would find their way into the right hands. Comenius in particular wrote to other teachers, as a practising teacher himself, faced with the problems of a classroom. Napoleon Bonaparte may be cred-ited with instituting the first serious training scheme for teachers. His *école normal* prepared chosen students for posts in leading French schools and universities. Shortly afterwards Pestalozzi began to train teachers to work in humbler situa-tions. Burgdorf and Yverdon were colleges as well as schools, in which future teachers were able to study the new methods, applied in a classroom situation. Pestalozzi himself felt that his experiment was a failure, and died a disappointed man.

But his German pupils continued to develop what he had started. The state of Prussia, which had long taken popular education seriously, instituted a three year training scheme for all those who intended to teach in state schools.

Reports of these Prussian colleges reached the attention of Horace Mann, Secretary of the Board of Education in Massachusetts, U.S.A. The common schools of his state were in a very low condition, and he reached the conclusion that sound teacher training was the prerequisite of any improvement. In 1839, therefore, the first Normal School for the training of teachers was opened at Lexington—the town in which the first shots of the War of Independence had been fired half a century earlier. On the day before the opening Mann wrote in his diary:

Much must come of it, either of good or ill. I am sanguine in my faith that it will be the former. But the good will not come of itself. That is the reward of effort, of toil, of wisdom. Neither time, nor care, nor such thought as I am able to originate shall be wanting to make this an era in the welfare and prosperity of our schools; if it be so, it will then be an era in the welfare of mankind.

The Lexington experiment prospered, and other American states opened their own normal schools. At about the same time the religious societies in England began to set up training institutions. Their student teachers were still, however, little more than children and it was not until the late 1840s that colleges sprang up which could compare with the American Normal Schools.

There was considerable opposition to the idea of teacher training. One of Horace Mann's critics argued that the experiment was a waste of money.

It is obviously impossible and perhaps it is undesirable that the business of keeping the schools should become a distinct and separate profession, which the establishment of these normal schools seems to anticipate.

He had, however, hit upon the very point which made Mann see his normal schools as the beginning of a new era. As long as teachers could be recruited from the refuse of other callings, there was no hope of improving their efficiency or their self respect. The professional status of the teachers sprang from the seed of Pestalozzi's experiment at Burgdorf.

By the middle of the nineteenth century there was still a vast gulf fixed between the humble teachers who were trained to work in schools for the poor, and the sophisticated scholars who ministered to the sons of the rich. The distinction can be best measured in hard financial terms. While a mistress in a school run by one of the English religious societies had to make do on £26 a year, her colleague serving as assistant master in a public school could expect to earn the princely sum of £800.

Until very recent times no public school would have welcomed a 'trained teacher' onto its staff. It was assumed that a degree in an academic subject at one of the ancient universities was the only proper preparation for service in a school for leaders.

During the past century the status of the college-trained teacher has improved, while that of the graduate has declined. Differentials of pay and career opportunity still exist, but there are few who would deny that both belong to the same profession. Broadly speaking the graduate offers subject specialisation at a higher level than his non-graduate colleague, but he has received less instruction in the specific skills of teaching, and so may find it harder to work with younger and less able children.

Teacher training is more essential than ever before, but there is a growing chorus of complaints from young teachers that their preparation did not fit them for the real problems which they faced when they took over responsibility for a class of their own. Some say that courses are irrelevant, others that lecturers are out of touch with the realities of school life. On occasions these critisims may be justified, yet it is hard for any college or department of education to train pupils adequately for a profession in such a rapid state of change. The freedom which was born of *Emile* and fostered by reformers opens up exciting possibilities for education, but can leave the inexperienced teacher feeling dangerously exposed in his classroom. Shorn of the status symbols of cap and gown, he must live among his pupils as one human being among others, and face up to all the problems which that entails. Many are puzzled about how they can use free methods which require individual attention for every child, when they are still asked to teach in oversize classes.

New demands on teaching skill pile up with bewildering rapidity, as each year produces some new shibboleth. Team teaching, mixed ability work, curriculum reform, language laboratories—the list could be continued. All offer opportunity for advances, but require the teacher to make constant assessment of his teaching method. It is already recognized that training can only be partially accomplished at the beginning of a teacher's career, and greater use will have to be made of in-service training, to enable practising teachers to bring their methods up to date.

Some may still manage to settle into a rut and 'perish of the same cabbage served up again and again', but before many years have passed they will be left, filling staff room chairs, like relics of some prehistoric era. Those teaching young children have to be able to assess and use new methods of putting over basic skills; subject specialists on the secondary level have to keep pace with discoveries and changes of emphasis within their particular disciplines. All have to meet new generations of children in a world of rapid social change—a world in which processes can now be worked out within a decade which would have hitherto taken centuries to develop. The teaching profession has been accused in the past of being inflexible and traditionalist in outlook. At times there has been justice in the accusation. Today the teacher, of all people, must be flexible in his thinking. He cannot judge new situations in the light of old dogmas—whether of Plato or Montessori.

It is a platitude but nonetheless true that the teacher's task is more urgent today then ever. The world's major problems are educational and, according to the President of the World Bank, unless rapid progress is made 'the world is going to remain explosively backward'.

All the technology and science known to man will have to be harnessed to feed the world's growing population. But starvation cannot be defeated on the technical level alone. If peasant farmers are going to plant the same crops as their fathers and grandfathers, using the same implements and the same techniques, then formal education can have little importance in their lives. Yet when scientists introduce new techniques they find this peasant mentality ill-equipped to cope with the demands of change. The basic technical discoveries which will increase world food production have already been made, but the task of educating the world's peasant farmers is far from being completed.

In colonial days missionaries and government officials were content to transplant western brands of education into Africa and Asia, with all their inbuilt assumptions and religious divisions. They were then puzzled that they did not flourish better in alien soil. Today new countries are building their own traditions. They are mostly glad to welcome teachers from countries with longer traditions of formal education and they have much to learn from the experience of the West.

It should not cause surprise if they look also to the East for inspiration. Communist education and technology has a record of solid achievement in a short period, which must appeal to teachers in developing countries. Without wishing to sacrifice their freedom to any ideology, they cannot but admire the sense of purpose which has been achieved in socialist countries. The school in which a child does his lessons, the factory in which his mother and father work, the home in which they come together to spend their leisure time are all closely integrated. Unfortunately in the West these are too often separate entities, uncoordinated in any common purpose. Politicians in the developing countries are faced with the brutal knowledge that their educational programmes must succeed or their countries will slip back into desperate poverty and unrest, which could spill over to endanger the peace of the world.

In the past, education has been used to erect barriers between nations. The time has now come for the role to be reversed, and for education to be used to break those barriers down. The American Negro was unhappily left out of the high school achievement of the late nineteenth century, and the 'great society' is today faced with desperate problems of race and poverty which ultimately can only be solved by education. But schools cannot undertake a single-handed battle against the prejudices of the wider community. Children pick up attitudes at home which cannot be erased in the classroom; teachers themselves are members of the society in which they live, and subject to the same pressures as other citizens. Fortunately the whole environment in

which our children live is growing larger, so that they become aware of other people, and their differences in outlook
and opinion. The teacher can use the techniques of his trade
to speed this process, so that pupils grow up understanding
what is involved in being a member of the human race at this
precarious period of its development.

One day in the House of Childhood in the slums of Rome
Maria Montessori told her pupils of a great earthquake
which had devastated the city of Messina. One of her little
pupils got up and walked to the blackboard. There he took a
piece of chalk and wrote the words 'I'm sorry'—then after a
pause he added 'I'm only little'. If he were big he would
have done something to help. This incident may seem to
provide a sentimental note on which to end the story of
teaching—yet it illustrates the deepest demand that can be
made on a teacher as a human being. The child had received
love, and so had love to spare for others. The relationship
between a pupil and his teacher is only second in importance
to that between a child and his parents. Multiplied over a
lifetime's teaching, the responsibility becomes truly alarming.

The man in the street rebukes the teacher when he
complains about levels of pay or conditions of work. 'Well,
it's a vocation, isn't it? You don't do it for the money.'
Within limits this is true, yet teachers will answer that no
amount of good-will and love for children can compensate
for lack of sheer professional skill. In centuries past teachers
have been recruited from those least fitted to meet the
emotional and intellectual needs of the young. Hardly more
than a century ago politicians could solemnly declare school-
mistresses to be well paid at £26 a year; having devalued the
profession it was easy enough to hold it in contempt.

Society undervalues the teacher at its own peril. Good
financial rewards and conditions of service are essential if the
standard of recruitment into the profession is to be maintained and improved. In assessing his own value the teacher
could well echo the words of John Dewey:

> I believe that the art of giving shape to human powers and
> adapting them to social service is the supreme art; one calling into
> its service the best of artists; that no insight, sympathy, tact,
> executive power, is too great for such a service.

Book List

─────

Educational thinkers are generally easier to understand when read in the original than when interpreted by other writers. A selection are :—

JOHN DEWEY. *Selected Educational Writings.* Heinemann Educational Books.

MARIA MONTESSORI. *The Secret of Childhood* (esp. Part 2, Chapter 2). Longmans, 1936.

A. S. NEILL. *Summerhill.* Penguin, 1968.

'PLATO'S *Republic* for Today'. Heinemann Educational Books.

JEAN-JACQUES ROUSSEAU. '*Emile* for Today'. Heinemann Educational Books.

HERBERT SPENCER. *On Education.* Dent Everyman Library.

Also for selected writings :

Readings in the History of Educational Thought, ed. Cohen and Garner. Univ. of London Press, 1967.

Fictional Reading :

CHARLES DICKENS. *Nicholas Nickleby* (Chapter 8: 'The Internal Economy of Dotheboys Hall').

THOMAS HUGHES. *Tom Brown's Schooldays.*

Women's Education :

ALICIA PERCIVAL. *The English Miss Today and Yesterday.* Harrap, 1939.

95

Historical Works. The immense literature on the history of education forbids any extensive book list. Serious students will be given one soon enough. An interesting start could be made on:

T. L. JARMAN. *Landmarks in the History of Education.* 2nd edn. Cresset Press, 1963.

For a sobering view of twentieth-century education:

JONATHAN KOZOL. *Death at an Early Age.* Penguin, 1968.

General works of reference:

WILLIAM BOYD. *A History of Education in the Western World.* 7th edn. A. & C. Black, 1964. (from the British point of view).

H. G. GOOD. *A History of Western Education.* 2nd edn. Macmillan, New York, 1960. (from the American point of view).

E. DE L. MYERS. *Education in the Perspective of History.* Longmans, 1963. (for non-Western civilizations).

Documents:

STUART MACLURE. *Educational Documents. England and Wales.* 2nd edn. Chapman & Hall, 1968.

Index